Retail Management, Retail Concepts and Practices

Dr. R. S. Tiwari

Director,
Bansal Management College,
Bhopal.

Himalaya Publishing House

ISO 9001:2015 CERTIFIED

First Edition : 2009
Reprint : 2015
Reprint : 2021

Published by : Mrs. Meena Pandey for **Himalaya Publishing House Pvt. Ltd.,**
"Ramdoot", Dr. Bhalerao Marg, Girgaon, Mumbai - 400 004.
Phones: 022-23860170, 23863863; **Fax:** 022-23877178
E-mail: himpub@bharatmail.co.in **Website:** www.himpub.com

Branch Offices :

New Delhi : "Pooja Apartments", 4-B, Murari Lal Street, Ansari Road, Darya Ganj, New Delhi - 110 002.
Phones: 011-23270392, 23278631; Fax: 011-23256286

Nagpur : Kundanlal Chandak Industrial Estate, Ghat Road, Nagpur - 440 018. Phones: 0712-2738731, Telefax: 0712-2721216

Bengaluru : Plot No. 91-33, 2nd Main Road, Seshadripuram, Behind Nataraja Theatre, Bengaluru - 560 020.
Phone: 080-41138821; Mobile: 09379847017, 09379847005

Hyderabad : No. 3-4-184, Lingampally, Besides Raghavendra Swamy Matham, Kachiguda, Hyderabad - 500 027.
Phone: 040-27560041, 27550139

Chennai : New No. 48/2, Old No. 28/2, Ground Floor, Sarangapani Street, T. Nagar, Chennai - 600 012. Mobile: 09380460419

Pune : "Laksha" Apartment, First Floor, No. 527, Mehunpura, Shaniwarpeth (Near Prabhat Theatre), Pune - 411 030.
Phones: 020-24496323, 24496333; Mobile: 09370579333

Lucknow : House No. 731, Shekhupura Colony, Near B.D. Convent School, Aliganj, Lucknow - 226 022. Phone: 0522-4012353; Mobile: 09307501549

Ahmedabad : 114, "SHAIL", 1st Floor, Opp. Madhu Sudan House, C.G. Road, Navrang Pura, Ahmedabad - 380 009.
Phone: 079-26560126; Mobile: 09377088847

Ernakulam : 39/176 (New No. 60/251), 1st Floor, Karikkamuri Road, Ernakulam, Kochi - 682 011. Phones: 0484-2378012, 2378016; Mobile: 09387122121

Cuttack : New LIC Colony, Behind Kamala Mandap, Badambadi, Cuttack - 753 012, Odisha. Mobile: 09338746007

Kolkata : 108/4, Beliaghata Main Road, Near ID Hospital, Opp. SBI Bank, Kolkata - 700 010. Phone: 033-32449649; Mobile: 07439040301

DTP by : HPH, Editorial Office, Bhandup (Shobha)

Printed at : M/s. Charita Impressions, Hyderabad on behalf of HPH.

PREFACE

The retailing has been in existence in the quite past however organized retailing is the recent phenomenon in Indian economy nevertheless it is growing at a pace which nobody has thought in the country. It is providing opportunity of employment to a large section of the people and making shopping a leisurely and entertaining activity. Although retailing is being practiced everyday retail management needs some theory and a few guiding principles.The characteristics of retailing are peculiar and every successful retailer has been able to develop a model which may be replicated with or without modifications.

The store management is one of the most complex exercise and retail marketing beings with understanding the shopping behaviour.The type of stores, its location and layout and supply chain are critical factors on the one side and consumer behaviour, the psychology of buying and macro level economic conditions on the other.

The book is intended to cover all these aspects in brief basically from the point of view of students of business schools. Various aspects of retail management at the introductory level are covered and explained in easy language to enable students to comprehend easily.The further analysis will be covered in the subsequent books but it serves the purpose of students by covering one of papers in their syllabus.The book is intended to serve as text book for the students.

I do not claim any originality in the book since most of the issues have been borrowed from the available literature. I am thankful to all those who have expressed views on the topics covered under the book. I am grateful to my family members who extended moral support to me in bringing this book.

R. S. Tiwari

Contents

Windows

Walls

Size

Construction and External Appearance

Entrances

Balance and Symmetry

Signs

Interiors

Proper Lighting

Music

Scent

Building

Displays

Good Outlay

Poor Layout

Desirable Layout

Information

Special Services

Personnel

Questions

CHAPTER 1

Retail

"A significant difference in today's marketing environment is the continuing concentration of buying power in many markets"

– Anonymous

INTRODUCTION TO RETAILING

Retailing is as old as exchange. Retailing is one of the oldest businesses in the world and was practiced in prehistoric times. Earlier it was the exchange of food and traditional weapon which followed the emergence of traders and peddlers. The day barter has been replaced by exchange through money (in any form) the retailing came into existence. In fact during barter also retailing was present in a sense however that was between two persons who were both the producers and consumers simultaneously. With the growth of division of labour and specialization the trade, business expanded and the retailing assumed significance. With the development of concept of market and marketing retailing started playing a vital role in growth of the economy. It is estimated that by 3000 BC shops came into existence. During the Greek and Roman period, a number of stores and something like specialty shops, developed in the form of open booths, where people from various countries use to have buying. By 14th Century retail trade assumed great importance. Merchants have started playing a crucial role in social political and economic life. A philosophy known as Mercantilism became popular in U.K. Italy, Holland and other European countries. Small stores, selling special line of goods became quite popular during 18th Century. The development of civilization, economic systems, modernization and consumerism the role and importance of retailing has been increasing and assuming various dimensions. India has a long history of trade and commerce and retailing in the traditional form has been prevailing since the ancient period. Now the organized retailing is gaining momentum and the globalization has opened vast opportunities for retailing.

What is this 'retail' thing anyway?

Lots of types of businesses, with very different requirements and different users are classified as *"Retail."* As a single category of modern real estate, retail includes businesses that serve everyday needs, such as groceries and drug stores, restaurants,clothing and apparel as well as stores that sell specialized products for narrow markets such as navigation equipment and supplies for aviators. Clearly these businesses have very different spatial and location requirements,but they all are selling goods and services to their end users.

Despite this variety, there are consistent patterns to the requirements of all retail.The two obvious and crucial elements to a successful retail business are a sufficient market, and visibility and access. Without a demand for the product or service, the retail endeavour is bound to fail. Likewise, if no one knows that it is there, or if it is difficult to get to, it will also face difficulties. Visibility is the most basic form of marketing. Locating on highly travelled routes suggests a market, visibility and access. In accordance with this, minimum daily traffic counts are often required by modern retailers; however high speeds are not very desirable since they reduce visibility and access to site. At the same time, extreme traffic congestion can be a deterrent to access and shoppers.

Trade in goods and services and lemonade has been the center of activity in cities for thousands of years. For most of history, retail services have located in cities to be close to concentrations of customers–this provided people with easy access to daily needs and a steady market for businesses.The demographic trends of the second half of the 20th century saw a shift in population as people moved to low density suburbs. The lemonade stand made a quick debut in the first ring suburbs and disappeared in the low density suburbs. In pursuit of this suburban market retailers were forced to adapt.

Retail is dead; long live retail: retail is an ever-changing business. The changes in the last sixty years represent a significant historical moment.

India's economic growth is an exciting and during last few years it has been hovering around 8% and increased to 9.4% during 2006-07. The opening of economy during 1991 helped the economy in a big way. Globalisation, privatisation and liberalisation have changed the entire growth story of the economy. 21st Century brought new dawn to India and now most of the countries including developed and developing ones are accepting that the future of India is bright and it is likely to emerge as economic power. By 2025 it is likely to become third largest economy of the World. The economic reforms have changed the nature and constitution of the economy. The agricultural economy of the country is now predominantly become service sector oriented. The share of Service sector in Gross National Product has now exceeded 55% (2007-08) and the trend continues.

The trade and commerce is increasing which is a natural corollary to high growth. The role of marketing has assumed significance in the process. The development in the field of technology, provisions of World Trade Organisation and spread of consumerism have given Phillip to marketing. A number of foreign companies are entering in the country to exploit the potential of Indian market With these Multinational Corporations, various new marketing strategy and practices also introduced in the country

Rising incomes, increased advertising, and a jump in the number of women working in the country's urban centers have made goods more attainable and enticing to a larger portion of the population. At the same time, trade liberalisation and more sophisticated manufacturing techniques create goods that are less expensive and higher quality. In this process, retailing got significant position and Retail has emerged as a big industry. In India, both the organised and unorganised retailing are prospering mean while there has been some opposition to organised retailing with the apprehension that it may harm traditional retailing and may result into increased unemployment, however organised retailing is getting momentum in a big way for its basic desired functions and contribution.

Emergence of a strong retail sector can contribute immensely to the economic development of any country. With a dominant retail sector, the farmers and other suppliers can sell their products directly to the major retail companies and can ensure stable profit.On the other hand, to ensure steady supply of goods, the retail companies can inject cash into the production system.This whole process can result into a more efficient production and distribution system for the economy as a whole. the Indian retail industry is expected to generate 10 to 15 million jobs by direct and indirect effects.This huge employment generation can be possible because being dependent on the retail sector shares a lot of forward and backward linkages.India is now prepared-to tap the enormous potential of the retail sector.Wal-Mart, the world's largest retailer, is interested in opening shops in India. Other popular brands like Pantaloons, Big Bazar (India), and Archies (U.S.) are rapidly increasing their market share in the retail sector.

RETAIL CONCEPTS

Retail as a concept– Retailing as an economic activity involves all the steps in which a product (goods and services) reaches to the final consumer after its production. It is a process of distribution channel. It finds place every where whether its a metro or a small village. In the process of distribution it is necessary that customer gets greater satisfaction and producer gets a reasonable profit by selling the product without building a huge inventory. The retailing concept has four pillars.

Customer orientation– It must be remembered that satisfaction of consumer/customer is the ultimate goal of all economic activity since any other activities, e.g., production, exchange, distribution are meaningless if they are not able to provide satisfaction to the consumer. It is therefore necessary that retailing is conducive to increased customer orientation. Retailer has to identify the needs, choices, preferences and likings of the customer. Moreover a retailer has to satisfy many other needs of the individual customer.

Coordinated effort– It is apparent that retailing is the last stage of the process in which any product is produced by various factors of production, thereafter it is marketed to reach to ultimate customer.In between there are distributor, wholesaler and a whole range of persons engaged in promotional activities.Then only the retailer emerges on the scene.Thus, it required coordinated efforts on the part of these channels. A failure in any of the link will frustrate the objective of customer satisfaction.

Value driven– Since only production does not lead to value addition, all other activities also add value to the product.The retailer provides many services which are unique to him and thereby results in value addition. Keeping various brands of a product helps customer in making choices, comparing price, qualilty and other features of the proudct and enables customer to get greater satisfaction. Sometimes various services 'exclusive to customer' are also provided by the retailer such as selling on personal credit, making home delivery, providng entertainment in a mall, etc.This is nothing but value driven approach which provides increased satisfaction to the customer.

Goal Orientation– Retailer helps producer in achieving its goal of increased sales, increased profit, enhancing share, building image of the product, etc. Retailer hleps in achieving the goal of producer, consumer as well as society at large. A suitble strategy is needed to be evolved by the retailer in accordance with the goal.

RELATIONSHIPMARKETING

In order to effectively use the retailing as a marketing tool, a retailer must have a definable identity to promote a clear positioning statement, so that key attributes can be translated into tangible elèments of store design and other supplementary services. With this defined personality, a program of activities can be assembled based on relationship marketing, which will include external advertising being reflected at point of purchase, i.e., the store.

Applying the Retailing Concept —

Customer Orientation → Retail Strategy → Coordinated Effort → Value-Driven → Goal Orientation → Relationship Marketing

A retailer has to plan space as a part of marketing strategy.What consumers see in any retailing is initially visual except in door-to-door selling.That is why the key to a store's marketing strategy is its identity and image. Strategic identity is a strong concept developed early on in the marketing positioning process,whether it's a new store or repositioning of an existing one.

Giving a name to the business, and its products and services is the most important factor in positioning. A say without any name and symbol will not capture the mind.That is why it needs to be memorable and thus marketable. Retailer witnesses a serious problem for giving a name and its positioning since he is not the producer of any product.

Retailers also need to consistently communicate unique points of view through decisive marketing environments in order to differentiate themselves from the competition.This may start with the three dimensional selling environment but also extends into all other components of the retail business, such as cards, people and management culture.

Definitions

Retailing: selling goods and services to consumers for their personal, family, or household use.Retailing is the *last stage* in the distribution process.

Wholesaling: an *intermediate stage* in the distribution process during which goods and services are not sold to final consumers but to business customers

Functions: Retailing has brought in phenomenal changes in the whole process of production, distribution and consumption of consumer goods all over the world.In the present world most of the developed as well as developing economies are using the retail industry as their vital growth instrument.In fact, the strength of the retail industry lies in its ability to generate large volume of transaction and perform various function which are essential for growth of economy and welfare of the people.

Retailing performs various functions in our day to day life. Its main role is seen in distribution channel of marketing.It serves producer, consumer and economy as a whole in a big way.

Producer– Retailer serves the producer/manufacturer in facilitating the distribution.The product may not reach to the needy customer in absence of proper retailing activities.The producer may develop a huge inventory which increases the cost and tell upon the profitability of the organization. He conveys the message of producer and promotes products by passing information to the consumer particularly in those cases where brand image and loyalty is not significant.

Consumer– Retailer is key to the availability and accessibility of the products to the consumer. Retailer offers the finished products to the customer at a proper place and proper time.Thus, he increases the utility to the customer.He provides choices to the customer since he stores variety of products at a place.The assortment of products in various categories help customer to select products of their choices and compare the value of various products.He also helps the customer in providing products at proper and convenient time by opening the shop.The location of the retail is very important to the customer.Moreover, retailer may provide many other services to the customer and consumer.The satisfaction and thereby happiness of the consumer depends largely upon the existence and service of the retailer.

Economy– The machining is possible through retailing and thereby the transactions take place in a big way generating Gross Domestic Product in the economy.The role of service sector is important in every economy including India. Retailer helps in providing link between producer and consumer thereby facilitates exchange.It also helps the economy by providing jobs to a large number of persons having high to low skills.He overcomes the problems of language, culture and life style of the people.

Service orientation– Since retailer has no control over the quality and nature of products, his interface with customer is predominantly service oriented. A retailer attracts and attaches customer through his service and behaviour.

Breaking Bulk This is one of most important function of the retailer. It should be remember that the meaning of retailing is nothing but breaking bulk.The producers transport the products in bulk to various locations to reduce cost whereas retailer put them in smaller quantity as per requirements of the customer

Assortment– Retailer offers opportunity and facility to select product of choice conveniently by assortment of merchandise. It requires large space, appropriate designing, layout and management of personnel. This function is unique to retailing.

Variety– The manufacturers or producers normally do not make variety of products (quite limited products with their brand name) and prefer to sell to small number of buyers to avoid high distribution costs and other problems involved with selling.On the other consumers buy small quantity of variety of products and want availability of these variety of products in desired quantity nearer to them.The retailer serves the interests of both of the above by procuring products from producers in a large quantity and by making variety available to consumers in nearby located store.These variety of products are available to customer in one store.

Inventory management– Since retailer has to satisfy large number of customer who buy small quantity of products and frequently, stock of various products is to be maintained in a reasonable quantity.Thus inventory management is critical since it increases the cost. By holding stock of variety of products at a time by the retailer helps the producer to produce cost of inventory in a big way.

Channel of communication– Products are produced as per the needs of the customer however producer and customer hardly meet ever. The retailer provide the channel of communication between the producer and customer.The feedback is communicated to the producer who changes the product as per needs of the customer. Retailer is the only person who can provide feedback to the producer since he is the person who come in contact to the customer and knows the mind of the customer more accurately.Thus production and marketing people get the accurate version of the latent demand of the customer.The marketing strategy is formulated on the basis of this feedback. Similarly the desired modifications and alteration are made at production stage .

Value addition– Retail plays a vital role in bringing balance between demand and supply in terms of quantity as well as quality, nature, size, etc. to provide greater satisfaction to the consumer.Thereby retail plays an important function of value addition both in goods and services.Philip Kotler while defining marketing observes that it is ***" the process by which individuals and groups obtain what they need and want through creating, offering, and freely exchanging products and services of value with others."*** is quite appropriate for retailing since all these functions are performed by retailing.

Customers are increasingly demanding relevant value propositions that meet their individual needs and preferences and will seek out those retailers able to provide them.This new environment requires a shift in thinking from ***"bell curves"*** to ***"well curves"*** – as growth and perceived customer value migrate to opposite ends of the competitive spectrum.

Accurate Forecasting – Rather than relying on the gut feel of a few individuals, retailer normally update forecasts based on early sales data, track and estimate forecast accuracy, test products and implement a blend of bottom-up and top-down forecasting. Example: SAGE Books retailer tracks sales by product category at each store, and periodically uses its merchandise planning system to automatically adjust each store's assortment.

Supply Chain Speed – One of the function of retailers is to improve supply chain responsiveness so as to reduce stock outs on hot sellers (popular items that sell out) and also to reduce markdowns because less merchandise needs to be ordered initially.

Additional Retail is a service and have details.Retailing ensures convenient availability, selection, ambience, quality, break bulk and certain services, e.g., alteration and credit. Some people finds retailing a therapy since it makes the customer happy and satisfied.The treatment given to customer is princely.

Retail is also treated as entertainment since it promotes fashion which has a shelf life.The quality of a product (including service is difficult to judge and mostly a guesswork for a customer but fashion is obvious. Excitement can be add in fashion by a retailer.

The first big one is the undisputable fact that almost all retail players (especially in food) have been region-specific. So whether it is FoodWorld, Nilgiris, Margin Free Market, Giant, Varkey's and Subhiksha in the South, Sabka Bazaar only in and around Delhi, Haiko and Radhakrishna Foodland which are Mumbai-centric; or Ahmedabad-based Adani, they have clearly battled with scalability.

But even scaling has multiple implications. Clearly, ideally it is an attempt to increase market share/ revenues or growth. But the question is: How does it affect operations? Does it mean reduction in assortment, shift to standardization and reduced customization? Where to scale, up, down or out? When to scale? Should a FoodWorld replicate its South-based format in a Delhi? And what happens when it wants to go to other 10 million+ towns? And then lower down the pop strata? Is it just a 'mini revolution?'Or a 'maxi' one? (More real estate space is available in smaller towns, but do the footfalls justify the bigger box format?)

Cross border transactions are normal now. Production may take place in one country and consumption may take place in other countries through retailer.

Today's customers are more informed, more discerning, with more choices and more power. They are more attentive to the benefits and consequences of consuming anything.

The framework of Retailing

Retailing = the sale of tangible goods + the sale of services

(haircut, airline travel, delivery.)

Retailing does not have to involve a store.(Mail, Phone orders, direct selling, web transaction). Manufactures, importers, non-profit firms act as retailers.Manufacturer may directly reach to retailer avoiding wholesaler, however in organized retail wholesaler is normally present.

Characteristics of Retailing

Retailing has a number of characteristics which are specific to it and make it a distinguished activity in the process of marketing. Retailing is a part of value chain and the process of marketing is not complete unless retailing takes place.Location is most important factor in retail business since it has to come into direct contact of innumerable consumers spread in the area.

The number of retail units are large enough since it has to ensure the accessibility of consumers in their close vicinity.The number depends upon the size and intensity of population alongwith the topography of the area.The identification of a proper location is difficult and establishing the store is costly business.The decision of location depends largely from the consumer point of view as against the economics and other rational factors.The number and size of retail store is determined by the needs and convenience positioning of the customers, the potential demand of products, supply of merchandise and positioning and image of the retail unit.

Direct contact with customers is another important feature of retailing.Retailer has a direct interaction with the ultimate customer of product.The producer of the product might be located far away even in other country but the retailer has to be near the customer by any means. Retailer is in direct contact of the customer and has to communicate with him.Therefore the cultural factors, language, tone, style and mode of communication are to be devised in consideration of the customer. A retailer thereby serves both the customers and producer since he is the promoter and advertiser of the product and can influence the total sales in a big way.

Promotional activities are performed by the retailer to a vast number of customers.In spite of various promotional measures, advertisement, propaganda and publicity, a large number of customers are unaware and uninfluenced by the product.Ultimately they are guided by the retailer who provides information about features and quality of the product, convince them and persuades them to buy a particular product.A number of customers are influenced by the display, presentation, posters in the retailer store, at the time they visit the shop store since they do not have any fixed shopping list, a fixed brand preference, a pre - determined need. The purchase in a number of cases is impulsive,unplanned and situational.Here, the displays,lay out of the store,categorization and assortment, visibility and marketing tactics of the seller play critical role particularly in products which are purchased in a small quantity,low priced and quickly consumable. Fashion products are sold in the similar manner in a big way.The role of retailer is critical here.

The average quantity of sales of products is relatively small as compared to wholesaler or producer. Mostly retailer sales products for household consumption. Many products are bought on daily, weekly or monthly basis.Thus the number of transaction for retailer are high with a low volume.This is a tremendous task since every day a large number of customers are to be handled by the retailer and a number of products are sold.The retailer has to maintain a reasonable stock of various products and the inventory management is critical here.

A number of activities are involved in the retailing. Besides behaviour of the seller, the packaging, timely service,credit verification,gift wrapping, convenient delivery, facility of buying back, prepare to change, various provision of guarantee and warrantee are involved in retailing. The customer orientation is critical factor in retailing.

The retailer's service many times is more important than the brand, quality and loyalty of the product.It is the loyalty and trust of the retailer which is more important. The growing world of retail has many features, where merchandising behemoths are no longer confined by domestic boundaries. According to the 2003, Global Powers of Retailing report by *STORES* magazine and Deloitte Touche Tohmatsu, four years ago more than half of the top 200 retailers in the world operated in only one country.That number has since dropped to 44 and by 2008 that has gone down to 30.

CHAPTER 2

Retailing Indian and Global Environment

Nobody including Indians have idea that India will emerge as an economic giant in many respect and the World will recognize its potential so soon. The economy has been growing at a rate above 8% in the recent past and so much so that Goldman Sachs, has estimated that the Indian economic growth could actually exceed that of China by the year 2015.

Indian economy has changed radically during post liberalization period–

- From a *shortage* economy of food and foreign exchange, India has now become a *surplus* one.
- From an agro based economy it has emerged as a *service oriented* one.
- From the low-growth of the past, the economy has become a high-growth one in the long-term.
- After having been an aid recipient, India is now joining the *aid givers* club

Goldman Sachs Report of 1 October, 2003 "Dreaming with BRICs: The path to 2050" says the following about the future of Indian economy. thereby becoming the third largest economy after USA and China India's GDP will reach to

$ 1 trillion by 2011,

$ 2 trillion by 2020,

$ 3 trillion by 2025,

$ 6 trillion by 2032,

$ 10 trillion by 2038,

$ 27 trillion by 2050,

Indian economy has been the second fastest growing economy after China in the world, the III largest economy in terms of GDP in the next 5 years and the 4th largest economy in PPP (Purchasing Power Parity) terms after USA,China and Japan,India is rated the most attractive destination for FDI (Foreign Direct Investment).

Inspite of a sudden shock during the second quarter of year 2008 because of high rate of inflation, the Indian economy is growing at a faster pace. During 2007 more than a third of India Inc. have achieved a "super growth" status as per Grant Thornton Survey.

Emergence of retail sector- Emergence of retail sector in such a big way that it will attract attention of all concerned is also surprising– but it is a fact.Retail has become a new buzzword here just like IT and mobile had become a few years back.Indian retail sector is exploding and is poised to get organized in a large way and is undergoing fundamental changes in nature and pattern from the existing one. Although we still visiting our neighbourhood kirana store, the organized retail too is alluring in a big way. AT Kearny,the well known international management consultancy in its recent report identified India as the "second most attractive destination"globally from among 30 emerging markets. It must be remembered that traditional unorganized retailing has a long history .

Retailing is poised to become one of the largest industries in India and the size of the economic activity in this industry is bound to have an impact not only on the consumers and manufactures but also the entire growth of economy.From mandi's to mall's, Indian retailing has come a long way. The transformation of Indian retailing is but to be noticed especially with Indian economy playing a crucial role globally.

India's retail industry accounts for10 per-cent of its GDP and 8 per-cent of the employment to reach $17 billion by 2010.There are about 300 new malls, 1,500 supermarkets and 325 departmental stores being built in the cities very soon.

According to Retail Industry estimates, the Indian Retail market is presently the fifth largest retail destination globally. It is estimated to grow from the US $ 330 billion in 2007 to US$ 427 billion by 2010 and as big as $ 637 billion by 2015. Presently, the share of organized retail is about 4% of the total market and estimated to increase to 22% within 3 years, i.e., by 2010. Organised retail is located mainly in metropolitan and other big cities whereas the small towns and villages where most of the population resides provide vast opportunity of its expansion.

The retail industry provides employment to around 8%of the population of the country and contributes over 10% to the Gross Domestic Product. It is expected to increase at the rate of 25% p.a.

At present, among all the industries of U.S.A. the retail industry holds the second place in terms of employment generation.Its ability to generate large volume of employment, in fact, is the strength of the retail industry besides increased satisfaction of the customers.

Not only U.S. but also the other developed countries like the UK, Canada, France,Germany and Australia are experiencing tremendous growth in their retail sectors.This boom in the global retail industry was in many ways accelerated by the liberalization of the retail sector Observing this global upward trend of retail industry, now the developing countries like India are also planning to tap the enormous potential of the retail sector.There also the liberalisation has helped retail sector in expanding its activities. Wal-Mart, the world's largest retailer,stook interest in opening shops in India.Other popular brands like Pantaloons, Big Bazar (India), and Archies (U.S.) are rapidly increasing their market share in the retail sector. According to a survey, within five years, the Indian retail industry is expected to generate 10 to 15 million jobs by direct and indirect effects.Forward and backward linkages of the retail sector are contributing to a great extent in generation of this huge employment.

Emergence of a strong retail sector contributes not only in employment genration but immensely to the economic development of any country. With a dominant retail sector, the farmers and other suppliers can sell their products directly to the major retail companies and can ensure stable profit.On the other hand, to ensure steady supply of goods, the retail companies can inject cash into the production system.This whole process can result into a more efficient production and distribution system for the economy as a whole.

Table -1

Retail Trade in India and South East Asia (%)

Country	Organised	Unorganised
Malaysia	50	50
Thailand	40	60
Philippines	35	65
Indonesia	25	75
South Korea	15	85
China	20	80
India	3.5	96.5

Source – Crisil and A.T.Kearney

Out of the BRIC countries, interestingly China and Russia are in the top 10 of the rankings while India and Brazil are lower down in the order.

In a global study conducted by real estate consultant CB Richard Ellis, India has been placed at number 44 in the list of preferred retail destinations.The survey entitled 'How Global is the business of Retail?' maps the global footprint of 250 of the world's top retailer.The report explores the globalisation of the retail industry and scrutinizes retailer presence in relation to market sectors, country of origin, regional trends and other influences.

The obvious reason for India's low rank despite the huge interest in Indian Organized retail has been the continued restrictions in FDI investments.There are a few additional impediments to the interest of India as a retail destination such as an immature supply chain system, complicated markets, and the rising real estate prices in the central places of cities.There have been till now no big local or international retail chains that have made huge success in the Retail Market despite some very heroic efforts by the Future Group.

The study ranks the UK as the current global leader in relation to international retailer presence, with 55% of retailers surveyed present. Spain's position as the second ranked market, closely trailing the UK, is an unexpected result which gives perspective to the market's new global significance, with 51% of retailers present.

Spain's growing ability to attract global retailers to its shores is fuelling its rise as a global retail destination and threatening the United Kingdom's title as the 'most international retail market' in the world, according to a new study by CB Richard Ellis.

France and Germany also performed strongly in the global ranking, achieving third and fourth positions respectively, and emerging markets including the United Arab Emirates, China and Russia all figured in the top 10.

The penetration of international retailers in these emerging markets is similar to that of much more mature economies, explained by a number of domestic political, economic and retail market idiosyncrasies.

The United States surprisingly registered outside the top 10, at number 11, with 39% of international retailers present in that market. CB Richard Ellis attributes this to the maturity, size and strength of its domestic retailers, which make it a market that only the strongest foreign retailers are able to break into.

The report also analysed which types or categories of retailers have the strongest international penetration,and found that luxury goods dominated international retail expansion,with almost 90% having a presence in more than 10 markets.

This was markedly more than grocery, food and drink retailers, with just 60% present in 10 or more markets, and the clothing, footwear and accessories retailers of which 54% were in more than 10 markets.

However, as the report illustrates, many of the luxury retailers are particularly well-known for their clothing ranges, such as Hugo Boss or Versace, reflecting the historical tendency for high fashion brands to be offered internationally. Least likely to 'travel' were the department stores, with only 5% represented in 10 or more markets.

Top 10 Fast-Moving Consumer Goods retailers, 2005

Sector Rank	Top 250 Rank	Company	Retail Sales (US$ billions)	Country of Origin
1	1	Wal-Mart	$312.4	US
2	2	Carrefour	$92.8	France
3	4	Metro	$69.1	Germany
4	5	Tesco	$65.9	UK
5	6	Kroger	$60.6	US
6	7	Target	$52.6	US
7	8	Costco	$51.9	US
8	10	Schwarz	$45.9	Germany
9	11	Aldi	$45.1	Germany
10	12	Rewe-Zentral	$44.0	Germany

Sources: published company data and Planet Retail

Top 10 Hardlines & Leisure Goods retailers, 2005

Sector Rank	Top 250 Rank	Company	Retail Sales (US$ billions)	Country of Origin
1	3	Home Depot	$81.5	US
2	13	Lowe's	$43.2	US
3	25	Best Buy	$30.8	US
4	35	IKEA	$18.8	Sweden
5	39	Staples	$16.1	US
6	42	PPR Group	$15.8	France
7	44	Kingfisher	$14.5	UK
8	46	Office Depot	$14.3	US
9	52	Dell	$12.2	US
10	56	DSG Int'l (Dixons)	$11.7	UK

Sources: published company data and Planet Retail

Top 10 Fashion Goods retailers, 2005

Sector Rank	Top 250 Rank	Company	Retail Sales (US$ billions)	Country of Origin
1	32	Federated Dept. Stores	$22.4	US
2	38	JCPenney	$18.8	US
3	40	TJX	$16.1	US
4	41	Gap	$16.0	US
5	45	KarstadtQuelle	$14.3	Germany
6	48	Kohl's	$13.4	US
7	59	Otto Group	$11.5	Germany
8	72	Limited Brands	$9.7	US
9	79	Millennium Retailing	$8.6	Japan
10	81	H&M	$8.4	Sweden

Sources: published company data and Planet Retail

Top 10 Diversified retailers, 2005

Sector Rank	Top 250 Rank	Company	Retail Sales (US$ billions)	Country of Origin
1	9	Sears Holdings	$49.1	US
2	43	El Corte Inglés	$15.8	Spain
3	47	Marks & Spencer	$13.9	UK
4	89	Lotte Shopping	$8.0	S. Korea
5	90	Kesko	$8.0	Finland
6	112	Tokyu	$6.0	Japan
7	137	Maxeda (Royal Vendex)	$4.8	Netherlands
8	140	Massmart Holdings	$4.7	S. Africa
9	144	LVMH	$4.5	France
10	145	Gr. Galeries Lafayette	$4.5	France

Sources: published company data and Planet Retail

The high growth rate of the economy over 9% in 2007-08, the growing urbanization, changing lifestyle and increasing number of young population is giving boost to Retailing. Rising incomes, increased advertising, and a jump in the number of women working in the country's urban centers have made goods more attainable and enticing to a larger portion of the population. At the same time, trade liberalization and more sophisticated manufacturing techniques create goods that are less expensive and higher quality.

Table-2

Size of organized Retail market (Rs.crs.)

Category	2001-02	2007
Large segments	8850	23109
Other segments	6050	12159
Non store retailing	1100	1939
Total organized Retail	16000	37216
The 4 Large segments		
Food Total	1800	7473
Chain stores	1500	6726
Single large stores & others	300	746
Clothing	4950	10423
Manufacturing retailers	1350	2715
Chain stores	1450	3919
Single large stores	2150	3789
Consumer durables	1650	3787
Manufacturing	650	1307
Chain stores	450	1373
Single large stores	550	1106
Book & Music	450	1426
Chain stores	200	498
Single large stores	200	498

Source- Changing Gears- Retailing in India- The Economic Times.

WHY INDIAN RETAIL GROWING ?

It is a hat-trick for Indian retailing – with India retaining the top spot in the global retail index chart for the third year in a row. Overseas investors may continue betting big on the Indian retail story, reports. Even the world's largest retailer– Walmart are all giving a thumbs-up to the Indian market. Endorsing that view is global consultancy – AT Kearny, which has placed India at the top of the list of 30 emerging retail markets, including Russia and China. This is because, over the year, 2006 India's country risk is down by 21.8% and its market attractiveness is up 23.5%, making it the best proposition for global retailers.The sector is clocking a 25-30% growth annually. That is why AT Kearny believes that over the next two years,India may retain its top spot as a preferred retail destination. India Organized Traditional Retail is amongst the fastest growing sectors in the country. India ranks 1st, ahead of Russia, in terms of emerging markets potential in retail and is deemed a 'Priority 1'market for international retail.

"In the last two years, a number of changes made in regulation around things like FDI in single brand retail, some changes in taxation laws, introduction of VAT across many states that are far more supportive of an organised mass retail environment,"(1) Not only global but domestic. Large and new players like Reliance and Subhiksha have grown aggressively over the year. So, there is a 10% jump in market saturation and the time pressure variable for India is up 5%.

In mature markets, Retail and Consumer sector companies are constrained in their ability to grow and maintain profit margins as a result of a number of factors-

(a) deflationary operating environment – which has further increased ,

(b) market saturation – the demand constraint has been observed,

(c) slowing population growth – a phenomenon of almost all developed economies,

(d) more discerning but less loyal consumers. The competition and awareness among consumers have made them dis loyal to a particular product.

(e) There are also the immediate concerns of growing competitive pressures,...........

1. Hemant Kumar, Principal of AT Kearney, 2007

(f) an increase in the number of alternative sales channels,

(g) a blurring of roles between suppliers and retailers,

(h) and — particularly for consumer product manufacturers — a shift in the balance of power to the retailers.

(i) heightened regulatory pressures as a result of US resultant Sarbanes-Oxley legislation which imply greater accountability and accuracy in the reporting of financial results under IFRS and US GAAP,

(j) Increased levels of corporate governance and Board involvement

(k) Stronger internal control documentation and a greater need for stronger risk management practices across the enterprise.

As a consequence, the strategic focus of the sectoris moving rapidly towards the emerging economies and expanding consumer markets of Asia and Central and Eastern Europe— China and India in particular — which offer new opportunities for growth through

(a) global sourcing,

(b) off-shoring

(c) and the development of modern retailing.

Global environment - Globalisation is a ".. a social process in which the constraints of geography on social and cultural arrangements recede and in which people become increasingly aware that they are receding." – Malcolm Waters (1995)

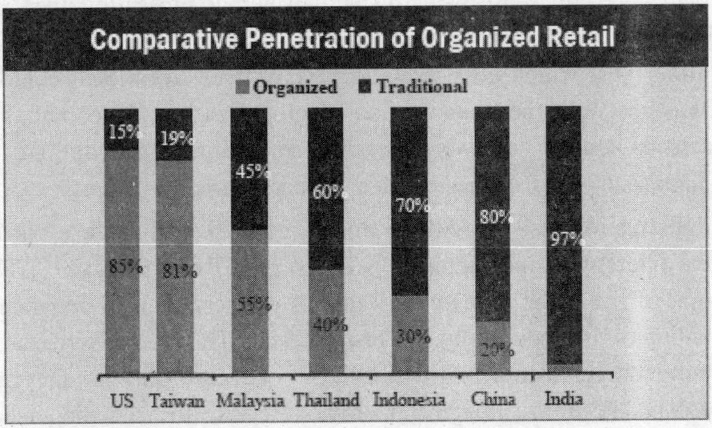

A t its most uncontroversial, globalization refers to the rapidly developing process of complex interconnections between societies, markets, cultures, institutions, and individuals worldwide.Globalization is a process that involves a compression of time and space, shrinking distances through a dramatic reduction in the time taken to cross them (either figuratively or literally), which in turn makes the world seem smaller, in a certain sense bringing human beings closer together. But globalization is also a process that 'stretches' social relations, removing the relationships, which govern our everyday lives from local contexts to global ones.With the phenomenon of globalization, no community/ culture is an isolate, and daily existence within most countries is increasingly enmeshed in these global processes and structures.

Globalization rests heavily on a view of the world as "one place," a matter inherent to individual consciousness (Robertson,1992).This perception of the globe as one site reminds of the imagined community of the nation, as introduced by Anderson (1983).This author writes, "all communities larger than primordial villages of face-to-face contact (and perhaps even these) are imagined.Communities are to be distinguished, not by their falsity/genuineness, but by the style in which they areat work within global communities.

imagined"(Anderson, 1990, p. 15).This imagination is certainly seen

It has great trust in the fact that economic freedom encourages competition and innovation.

It is based upon following

- ✦ Economic Efficiency at the maximum.
- ✦ Existence of Competition
- ✦ Unfettered market. Relationship – no barriers either from government or from social factors.
- ✦ Self interest is the key of success
- ✦ Economic Values are important instead of social values.
- ✦ What is good to market is also good for the society.
- ✦ Government to provide environment for and above and not to intervene.

Globalization– has resulted in following good to the society

- ✦ Greater integration into world economy.
- ✦ More openness.
- ✦ Market strategies Reaching to heart than to mind.
- ✦ Expansion of trade and cooperation.
- ✦ Diffusion of technology, particularly IT has brought revolutionary change and spread throughout the World.
- ✦ Extensive migration, particularly IT engineers, BPO personnel, service sector workers.
- ✦ Availability of goods and services globally without any obstacles and extra cost.
- ✦ No scarcity since accessibility has increased.
- ✦ Many goods become cheaper– e.g., mobile
- ✦ Old is no more gold.
- ✦ Wars became redundant.
- ✦ Wealth multiplied, wealthy increased.

Retailing got a big jump in the global system and perhaps it is the most benefited sector. Globalisation gave birth to global market place and that has fuelled the growth of retail across the world.

UNDER GLOBAL RETAILING

Intertype Competition – Similar stores selling the same basic product, e.g., Wal-Mart vs. Kmart; Rite-Aid vs CVS.

Intertype Competition – Different type stores selling the same product. e.g., Wal-Mart, Walgreens, Kroger all selling Crest toothpaste

Vertical Competition – Retailer competing with wholesaler or manufacturer, e.g., Shoe store selling Reebok's and Reebok factory outlet in Burbank system Competition — Competition between vertical marketing systems — e.g. McDonalds vs. Burger King.

In a global study conducted by real estate consultant CB Richard Ellis, India has been placed at number 44 in the list of preferred retail destinations. The survey entitled 'How Global is the business of Retail?' 2008 maps the global footprint of 250 of the world's top retailers. The report explores the globalisation of the retail industry and scrutinizes retailer presence in relation to market sectors, country of origin, regional trends and other influences. Out of the BRIC countries, interestingly China and Russia are in the top 10 of the rankings while India and Brazil are lower down in the order.

The obvious reason for India's low rank despite the huge interest in Indian organized retail has been the continued restrictions in FDI investments.There are a few additional impediments to the interest of India as a retail destination such as an immature supply chain system, complicated markets, and the rising real estate prices in the central places of cities. There have been till now no big local or international retail chains that have made huge success in the Retail Market despite some very heroic efforts by the Future Group.

The study ranks the UK as the current global leader in relation to international retailer presence, with 55% of retailers surveyed present. Spain's position as the second ranked market, closely trailing the UK, is an unexpected result which gives perspective to the market's new global significance, with 51% of retailers present.

Spain's growing ability to attract global retailers to its shores is fuelling its rise as a global retail destination and threatening the United Kingdom's title as the 'most international retail market' in the world, according to a new study by CB Richard Ellis.

France and Germany also performed strongly in the global ranking, achieving third and fourth positions respectively, and emerging markets including the United Arab Emirates, China and Russia all figured in the top 10.

The penetration of international retailers in these emerging markets is similar to that of much more mature economies, explained by a number of domestic political, economic and retail market idiosyncrasies.

The United States surprisingly registered outside the top 10, at number 11, with 39% of international retailers present in that market. CB Richard Ellis attributes this to the maturity, size and strength of its domestic retailers, which make it a market that only the strongest foreign retailers are able to break into.

The report also analysed which types or categories of retailers have the strongest international penetration, and found that luxury goods dominated international retail expansion, with almost 90% having a presence in more than 10 markets..

This was markedly more than grocery, food and drink retailers, with just 60% present in 10 or more markets, and the clothing, footwear and accessories retailers of which 54% were in more than 10 markets.

However, as the report illustrates, many of the luxury retailers are particularly well-known for their clothing ranges, such as Hugo Boss or Versace, reflecting the historical tendency for high fashion brands to be offered internationally. Least likely to 'travel' were the department stores, with only 5% represented in 10 or more markets.

Competitive pressures, especially the pressure on sales growth and profit margins, are encouraging companies of all types to pursue globalisation through M&A and industry consolidation.The availability of information technology and data capabilities have made serving and sourcing from global markets easier, thus permitting the adoption of new consumer products includes many layers like carrying and forwarding product and sales strategies, economic models and inventory management techniques to fuel growth. Consolidation, resulting in greater operational efficiencies and economies of scale, is shaping the retail industry and is seen as a way of strengthening one's position in an industry with fewer, larger players.

The global sourcing of products and the concentration of power within the industry are two factors affecting all retail and consumer companies. Suppliers are under pressure to deliver cheaper priced products and to deal more efficiently with retailers, who want to deliver everyday low prices. Global sourcing and acquisitions have been both a response and an outcome. In turn, retailers needing to increase sales and profit margins are expanding to global markets and consolidating to realise greater power in dealing with their suppliers.

Retail chains are among the most visible and criticized agents of globalization. They standardise their operations as far as possible and end up undermining the visibility of genuinely diversified independent retailers. International expansion is seen as a viable option for supermarkets in terms of increasing growth potentials.Such expansion is widely criticized since it invades indigenous entities with controversial impacts.Many studies prove that retail chains have devastating net effect on local producers, environment, labour and economy as a whole.The paper examines options chosen by states which try to hinder domination of global retail chains.

INDIAN RETAIL ENVIRONMENT

According to 2007 year's Global Retail Development Index India is positioned as the leading destination for retail investment.This followed from the saturation in western retail markets and we find big western retailers like Wal-mart and Tesco entering into Indian market.For retailing, Indian environment is most congenial since last few years.

Retail industry in India is greatly fragmented comparing to the developed and other developing countries.This presents enormous prospective for the structured retail industry to flourish throughout the country, as the market for the final product is huge.Retail industry is largely led by private companies.The distribution for fast-moving agencies, distributors, wholesalers, stockiest and retailers.

The global retail giants like Wal-Mart, Gap, Tesco, Versace, K-Mart/ SEARS, Carrefour, ZARA,FCUK,Fendi,NEXT, Mother Care,IKEA, Trussardi, DKNY and Debenhams either have already entered or have made plans to march in the Indian market. ESPRIT,GUESS,Chanel, Mango and many other global marked their presence in India by implementing licensing and franchisee agreements. Many global retailers on the line of control, awaiting the green signal from Government in certain areas to enter Indian retail market. However, the current scenario has encouraged Indian players to speed up retail expansion and fresh retail ventures.The unexpected high rate of inflation too gave opportunity to organized retailing since some Retailers are in position to sell certain products at a lower rate than Kirana stores. As per Earnst & Young report 2005, there were about 12 million retail outlets spread across India, earning it the epithet of a "nation of shopkeepers." More than 80% of these 12 million outlets were run by small family businesses which use only household labour. Traditionally, small-store (kirana) retailing has been one of the easiest ways to generate self-employment, as it requires limited investment in land, capital and labour.Consequently, India has one of the highest retail densities in the world at 6% (12 million retail shops for about 209 million households).

The India Retail Report 2007observes that the total private consumption touched Rs.20,000 billion (appx.$ 445 bn) during 2006 with organized sector accounting for Rs.55,000 crs. ($ 12.4 bn.).The total Indian Retail business is valued at Rs.12,0000 bn. ($270 bn.) and thus the share of organized retail accounted for 4.6% .This report projected the growth of organized retailing in the country at the rate of about 37% in 2007 and 42% in 2008.Retail industry attracted huge investment exceeding Rs. 200 bn.($4 bn.) in developing infrastructure, systems and shop fit.

It additional retail space is expected to add Rs. 300 bn. (6.67 bn.) of business to organized retail. It has the potential to add over Rs. 2,000 bn. ($45 bn.) business by the yaer 2010.With the change in lifestyles and buying habits of Indian consumers, the people look for ways to spend their money. Global retailers keep an eye on this and they are looking expected to increase to 32% by 2010. Disposable incomes are expected to rise at an average of 8.5% p.a. till 2015.

for prime locations. Since the market of advanced countries of West is saturated, the global retailers are finding India as the "promised land" for he global brand and retailers.

Environment boosting Retail sector

A number of factors are creating an environment for fast expansion of retailing in India. There is hectic activity in the sector in terms of expansion, entry of international brands and retailers as well as focus on technology, operations and processes. It is the economic, demographic and social environment which are encouraging retail to consider India as the best place for entry and expansion of retailing.

ECONOMIC ENVIRONMENT

Economic growth– Indian economy has been growing on an average of more than 8% during last 3 years and over 6% since last few years and consumer demand has been driving economic as well as retail growth. Needless to emphasise that economic growth results in higher level of income thereby increase in demand and further expansion of needs of the consumers and opportunity to the producer/supplier. Overall, it improves the environment for trade and transactions.

Spending capacity –This has meant greater disposable incomes for the booming Indian middle class, which currently comprises 22% of the total population.This figure is expected to increase to 32% by 2010. Disposable incomes are expected to rise at an average of 8.5% p.a. till 2015..

Conspicuous consumption– It is not only the necessaries but demand for comforts and luxuries increases with increase in income.It changes the psychology of the consumer and they tend to spend more and more to improve their standard of living and change life style. Indians with an ability to spend over USD30,000 a year (PPPterms)on conspicuous consumption represent 2.8% of the entire population. But with a population base of 1.07 billion people, this number amounts to 30 million people, a market next only to USA, Japan and China.:This has meant greater disposable incomes for the booming Indian middle class, which currently comprises 22% of the total population. This figure is

THE AFFLUENCE

The growth story has a dramatic positive effect on the economy and emergence of a increased number of affluent? India has 209 million households, of which the 6 million classified as 'rich' have annual incomes of over USD 4700 and 75 million classified as 'consuming' have annual incomes between USD 1000-4700. An estimated 1 million households at the top of India's income map constitute the 'super-rich' in the country.Over half of these 'rich' families live in Delhi, Mumbai and Bangalore, and spend around USD 18 billion annually. Growing by 20% every year, this segments' buying behaviour is in line with its corresponding international segments. While this segment is worth targeting for high-end premium products, it is not the key driver of the organized retail sector. It is estimated that 7 crores Indians earn a salary of over Rs. 8 lakhs (appx. $18,000) a year, and it is likely to double by 2010.The number of effective consumers is likely to cross 60 crs. by 2010.This makes India as one of the largest consumer market of the world.

URBAN POPULATION

Urbanization:

High economic growth and development model are encouraging urbanization and incomes are simultaneously expected to grow in these segment. Over half of these *'rich'families* live in Delhi, Mumbai and Bangalore, and spend around USD 18 billion annually.

62% of the market for premium products in India is also concentrated in these three cities. It is worth pointing out that 85% of India's retail market are located in the country's 8 largest cities. The top 6 Indian cities – Mumbai, Delhi,Chennai, Kolkata, Bangalore and Hyderabad -are the darlings of India's exploding economy.They represent 6% of the population, but contribute 14% of India's GDP. These cities are also the barometer of India's economic development and most foreign investors have flocked here.

SOCIAL ENVIRONMENT

(1) ———— See Ernst and Young – Report - The Great Indian Retail story, 2005.

CREDIT CULTURE

Credit availability:

Retail loans have doubled in the last three years.The change in the banking and buying habits have promoted hire purchase and use of credit cards. This has helped consumer in buying without having cash in hand. Since 2003 onwards the bank credit has became quite cheap, the availability increased, and a number of schemes allowing customer to make payment in installments, introduced by the suppliers, have developed an environment for growth and success of retailing.

Luxury – The attitude towards luxury has changed radically. Even middle income group people are prone to it.

Demographic Environment- The large young population has changed the attitude towards marketing.**Generation Y** is responsible for organized retailing to a great extent in the country.

As is known that India is a country of young since more than 50% of the population is less than 25 years of age and strong growth is expected to continue in this age bracket.The younger population has a natural tendency towards conspicuous consumption.This generation Y has a number of typical characteristics.It wants to live in present and wants to consume everything available, today itself without waiting further.

Women consumer-The increasing number of women is now earning. Thus nuclear families having atleast two members earning and freedom to women have made women one of the biggest buyer as well as consumer.They want to utilize their time, money and efforts in a manner which provide them satisfaction and distinctiveness.The organized retail got a big boost from this category of customer.

Children and Kids- Studies show that children and kids are more responsible for influencing buying decision.

Life Style

The social environment has changed radically during last few years. The life style of the people has changed as a result of pressure of work, desire for entertainment and leisure and improved standard of living.This changed life style demands various products and services either near to their home or delivery at home.Many retailers have emerged because of this new life style whether beauty parlor for men and women, fast food to many durable goods shops,several new services became popular. Retailers are interested in taking advantage of this environment.

Culture

A definite cultural change is noted in India.The Western culture which is market and consumption oriented is regarded as a sign of progress and modernization.The Retailers are trying to cloan the western mall culture in India and that is gaining success.

Fashion

Electronic media particular television is responsible for spreading new fashions evolved through fashion shows, bollywood and Hollywood and other shows. Even small towns are having beauty competition and fashion shows. Retailer have an edge over other traditional pop and mom shops since they can have a variety as well as large quantity of stocks at a time.Since fashion is changing at a faster pace, big retailers only can cope up with this.

CHANGE OF INDIAN MINDSET

- *Fatalism and contentment — to optimism and ambition.*
- *Introvert and defensive approach — outward-looking and confident attitude.*
- *denial and sacrifice, the Indian value — seeking of satisfaction and happiness*
- *wealth as a sin and believed in simple living and high thinking, — recognizing prosperity and success as acceptable and necessary goals.*

the total market within the coming four years, generating new 8mn jobs, in addition to the 21mn jobs that are already created by retail sector.

The environment in India is most conducive for the development of organized retailing. A shopping revolution is ushering in India where,

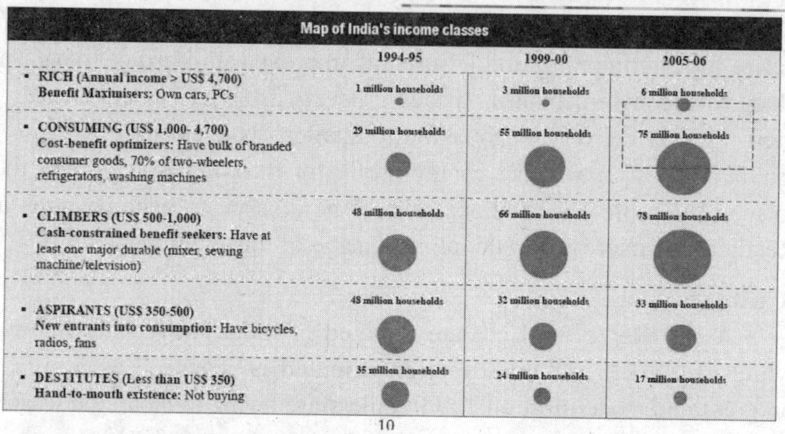

a large population between 20-34 age groups in the urban regions is boosting demand by about 13% per-cent per annum during 2003-08. This has resulted in huge international retail investment and a more liberal FDI alongwith big domestic companies like Reliance Fresh, Big Bazar, etc.

A combination of increased consumption and an under-developed organized retail environment has made India an attractive destination for global retailers. However, India's attractiveness has dropped from 100 to 92, on a scale of 100, during 2007

This is because new players have entered the market and the window of opportunity is getting smaller over time. Inspite of this, the potential for organized retail sales is high because of the upswing in young India's spending power.

The Indian retail environment has attained $ 210bn quiche, witnessing a strong development pace of five percent per year (according to a latest survey by Price Waterhouse Coopers). As per the estimation 200 malls, presenting additional 50mn sq. ft. of retail space will be ready in next two years. Existing retail space in 160 malls is nearly 32mn sq. ft.

Organized retailing now accounts for three per-cent out of the total retailing, however is predicted to extend to 10 per-cent by the year 2010. In other means, organized Indian retail sector would triple its share of

As per the estimate, the current retail business witnesses more than 12mn retail outlets, which include all shapes and formats.

The analysts foresee bright future of the retail sector. A huge number of shopping malls, nearly 100, have come up in the recent past, generating 20mn sq. ft. retail space, extending more space of about 12mn sq. ft. to it. Nearly 60 malls are on the verge of completion and may be operational by the end of current financial year. A forecasted number of nearly 200 malls, in a move to make additional 50mn sq. ft. of retail space, will be completed within the next two years.

According to analysis by KSA Technopak,India has lowest per capita retail space accessible around the globe.The study depicts that India require generating at least 110mn sq. ft. of additional retail space a year for many years, only to meet the demand generated on account of a continued GDP growth rate of nearly 6 per-cent. Hitherto, the Central Government as well as State Governments and local municipals have failed to match steps with drag on the economy of an incompetent retail sector. This space crisis is leading to a condition, in which prime locations demand extremely high rates.

To make India's emerging retail market open to foreign direct investment (FDI) has been on the Government agenda since long time. A number of transformations and practices were being done, but the sources disclosed that the policy, which is under finalization is such that FDI in the retail market would lead towards the rear connections of manufacturing and production and not only set aside to open of retail stores of global and imported brands.

Companies like Shoppers Stop,Trent, Reliance, Lifestyle,Tanishq, Crossroads, Akbarallys' and Tanishq already have planned to invest over Rs. 5,000cr. Trent is on the edge to take both its brands 'Star India Bazaar'and 'Westside' to new cities, meanwhile Shoppers' Stop has recently geared up for expansion of present ones and to add 11 new stores including two hypermarkets. Also, Pantaloon has planned to add eight 'Big Bazaar' malls within the next 6 to 8 months.

stores have completed setting up their back-end systems. So they are ready for Versa POS, which will handle their front-end operations.

After demerger, Reliance Industries Ltd (RIL) is substantially getting ready to enter in field of retailing. RIL is poised to emerge as the single largest player in this sector.On the other hand,Tescos, Wal-Marts or Safeways ultimately enter in the country. So finally, Shoppers' Stops, Westsides, Pantaloons and Westsides in coming years have will face stiff competition. More than the Tescos and Wal-Marts, Reliance, Godreg and Tata are likely to attain reach to the country's interiors.At the same time, several apparel exporters are keen to get opportunities in retail sector. Gokaldas Images, OC,TCNS, Gokaldas Exports and Celebrity Fashions are some of the exporters who already have expanded into retail sector with triumph.

India, in fact, has scored behind Russia, China, Chile, Mexico and Argentina among other countries on market attractiveness, which was one of the four criterion used for the global retail development index.

This market research report "The Indian Retail Sector – An Outlook (2005-2010)" analyzes the greatly divided Indian retail market and the trends in its business.Issues such as foreign investment restrictions, modern merchandizing in India, logistics and payment terms for distribution, role of channel members and growth trends in different regions are discussed. The market research report further analyzes the sustainability of the Indian retail sector and on the basis of 25 domestic and international companies the report has given a suitable business model.

Opportunities in the Indian retail market

The Indian retail segment is one of the largest in the world but has a long way to go as far as organised retailing is concerned. A joint report by McKinsey and the Confederation of Indian Industry (CII) has pegged the Indian retail market at $180 billion.The market, according to the report, is growing at a steady rate of 11-12 per-cent and accounts for around 10 per-cent of the country's GDP. Most retail customers today use Bradma-based Cash-Track register machines or the Casio cash register. Being completely unorganised, no data capture is being done. But with smart cards and credit cards finding huge acceptance with the populace, the need for retail applications is coming in. Most of the larger

Foreign retailers have identified two levels in the retail segment where they see huge growth opportunities—shops like Akbarally's and Shopper's Stop which have branches across the country and small chain stores found in most metros. They feel that their products can also be used in standalone stores with large operations. Most of the shoes and apparel stores in the country, especially in the smaller towns and cities, belong to this category.

REPORT HIGHLIGHTS –

- ✦ Competitive analysis of Indian retail sector *vis-à-vis* global retail industry.
- ✦ Supportive policies and regulations of government for the retail sector.
- ✦ Issues and implications related to the current foreign direct investment in the retail sector.
- ✦ Market size and growth of Indian retail sector segmented by sectors, retail formats, and regional segmentations.
- ✦ Increasing employment opportunities with stepping up of international retail brands in India.
- ✦ Opportunities for big western retailers like Wal-Mart and Tesco.
- ✦ Market forecast till 2010.
- ✦ Behavioural pattern, preferences and expenditure capacity of Indian consumers.
- ✦ Increasing acceptance of e-retailing among Indian consumers.
- ✦ Evolution of franchise businesses in Indian retail sector.
- ✦ IT trends in Indian retail industry and technological expansion leading to the stores' Security.
- ✦ Company profiles of 25 key players, which include 6 international retail brands.

Riding on Asia's robust retail growth and India's unprecedented retail boom, Jones Lang LaSalle Incorporated (NYSE: JLL), and Colonial First

State Property Management today announced a joint venture partnership to form Asia's first integrated retail development and management service provider? Sandalwood. The 50:50 joint venture company will help Asian and Indian developers and retailers to capitalize on premium retail opportunities as well as creating long -term value for retail assets.

Colonial First State Property Management is one of Australia's largest full service property development, management and leasing specialists. Since its inception in 1983, the firm has undertaken more than 25 major shopping centre developments and now manages 36 centres on behalf of third party clients in every state of Australia, including iconic Chadstone Shopping Centre in Victoria, Chatswood Chase in Sydney and Queens Plaza in Brisbane.

There are over 100 malls operating in India and more than 300 being developed and of this total, more than 90% have yet to achieve global benchmarks. In order to be globally successful, mall owners and developers in India need to focus on vision, scalability and processes and create a distinct proposition for themselves in this emerging market. Sandalwood, with its specialist property management skills and development expertise will ensure that retail owners and developers are strategically positioned for long term growth and success.

Anuj Puri, Chairman and Country Head, Jones Lang LaSalle Meghraj says, "As retail in India grows at a rapid pace, this is indeed an opportune moment for us to introduce specialized retail and intensive asset management services. Sandalwood will seek to create long term value for India's mall owners through its globally benchmarked practices, proven expertise in property development and intensive asset management."

Darren Steinberg, Head of Colonial First State Property Management says, "Asian economies are amongst the fastest growing in the world with real GDP compound average growth of approximately 9% per annum over the last five years, and their retail management and property development markets have grown at a compound average growth rate of more than 20% in the same period. Colonial First State Property Management's specialist retail property management skills enable property owners to receive the benefit of master planning and development expertise which is critical to ensuring assets are enhanced and strategically positioned for long-term growth and success."

Retailers are excited by the opportunities that lie ahead in India.The retail business in India is growing and the pace is expected to accelerate. The market and business outlook is extremely positive.

Jones Lang LaSalle has over 50 years of experience in Asia Pacific (ASPI.BO, news), with over 16,000 employees operating in more than 70 offices in 13 countries across the region.

Forms of Competition

With the advent of the internet and explosion of e commerce across borders in the 21st century, global firms will adapt their value chain philosophies to capitalise on cost efficiencies and strengthen their sustainable competitive advantage. This study illustrates the application of Rayport and Sviokla's three-stage Virtual Value Chain (VVC) philosophy to Wal-Mart, the world's largest retailer. Value chains using information technology allow managers and suppliers/vendors to track operations more effectively, with a holistic and integrated approach to managing information seamlessly. The focus of the VVC in the new economy is on information, unlike physical supply chain management where the focus was on inventory management. This applies the three stages of the VVC to Wal-Mart, including visibility – entailing tracking of physical operations via information; mirroring capability – substituting virtual activities for physical ones in the market space realm, and creation of new customer relationships using information. In particular, the authors focus upon the name of the game in supply chain management for the 21st century – collaboration among channel partners, information sharing and improved efficiencies in the value chain delivery network. Finally, this paper examines Wal-Mart's physical value chain activities and the emerging VVC, as the company considers expansion globally into emerging markets.

RETAIL OPPORTUNITIES AND CHALLENGES

Retailing is an important segment of Indian economy.This economic activity is both growth promoting and employment generating. Being labour intensive its contribution in creating opportunities for employment is quite high.The organized retailing which is hovering around 3% of the total has a great potential of contributing to GDP as well as employment level of the economy,which was not possible for unorganized retailing.

Although the emergence of organized retailing witnessed a hostile atmosphere and opposition from traditional sector, the shopping mall culture has been welcomed initially in Metros to be spread in other cities within a short period.The continued high economic growth and the growing middle class have given spurt to organized retailing in the country.

During the year 2008, there are plans for opening more than 150 malls and growth of about 24% of departmental store is expected.

Opportunities

Inspite of high rate of inflation and slowing down in certain sectors and slump in the share market, retail sector is poised to witness a high growth and by 2010 it is estimated to be of the order of Rs.12.5 trillion. The share of organized retailing will go up to about 10%. Both domestic and foreign players are entering in the sector in a big way and further planning to enlarge the operation.

* The high and continuous growth of population is alluring orgnaisations in this sector. A huge population of about 114 crores.With more than 30% urban and 60% adopting or keen to adopt new life style are providing vast opportunities for retailing.The favourable demographic is opening further scope for the growth of this sector.

* Organized retail is mostly banking upon growing urban middle class having income more than ....which is increasing at a fast rate in the economy.

* Unorganized retail mostly catering to the needs of lower income group, traditional families and rural segment. There seems no danger to this sector since the customers are constantly increasing for both the sectors.

* The organized retailing is growing fast because of the changing lifestyle and rising disposable income of the people.

* Recently, a number of organized retailers are trying to grab customers of small towns and villages too. In fact rural market is quite attractive since there are around 16 lakh households in rural India that come under the high income group. A number of surveys found that rural areas have the capability to spend around Rs.700 bn.on Fast Moving Consumer Goods (FMCG). The Study reveals FMCG products account for 53% of the rural market.It is estimated that the number of middle and high income households in rural areas would rise to about 11.1 crores. and rural India is now double the size of urban India.

* Now retailing is moving towards northwards in a big way and even less developed states are witnessing growth of organized retailing. This opens vast scope for retail industry in the country.

* The organized retailing has a distinct advantage of determining price particularly lower than traditional shops since organized retailing is undertaken in a large volumes, the price margin provides retailers with the opportunity to shape their pricing as per the market expectations.

* There is scope of penetrating in vast rural areas and with the low income class for organized retailing since besides convenience buying, the organized retail can provide many products cheaper than traditional stores.

* The penetration of Television and other media has helped in reaching to the people in the remote areas and making them aware of new products and transferring knowledge in many respects thereby the scope for retailing is expanded.

* The foreign big companies like WalMart, Marks and Spencer, and many giants are entering in India after conducting deep market research which indicated bright future for retail in this country. Many are coming in collaboration with Indian giants.

* Various studies suggest that Indian retail sector is going to reach the level of $637 bn. By 2015 from the present $330 bn.The share of organized retailing will go up to 18% in another 5 years.Thus, it is

estimated that the organized retail would gain somewhere between $10 bn and $ 50 bn. Within a period of 10 years which is not possible anywhere else.

Thus opportunities are galore for the retail industry in India.

Challenges

Indian retail industry is highly fragmented in nature and has the highest density.The unorganized retailing has a distinct advantage of having personal touch and emotional customer relationship. But for this, it has a number of problems.

(a) The existence of fragmented real estate sector.

(b) Inefficient upstream processes

(c) Poor infrastructure

(d) Lack of advanced technology

(e) Absence of proficient manpower

(f) Financial constraints.

(g) Lack of convenience shopping.

This has provided opportunity to organized retailing, however the new retail concepts like convenience stores and hypermarkets have a insignificant presence in the country. Although the growth is taking place, their share is not impressive as yet. A number of issues are there which act as challenges before Retail sector.

INFRASTRUCTURE CONSTRAINTS

Inspite of reiteration of special focus on infrastructure in the country by policy makers, still the country is lagging much behind to developed countries.Currently, highway network of less than 2% bears 40% of the traffic.The State highway network is of limited length.The completion of "Golden quadrilateral"is still a distant goal Transport connectivity is a serious problem.

- **Logistic problems**

  Retailing has always facing this problem even in advanced countries. The lack of distribution channels linking towns other than Class I is a big constraint. Absence of linkage with local logistics centres is a major bottleneck.Due to increased rip-off the operational cost increases.The CMIE estimated that the total cost of logistics in the country is somewhere between 10% and 12% of the GDP

- **Weak Supply chain**

  Information Technology (IT) can help achieve great benefits in terms of the agility and visibility of the information flow. But increased systematic coordination across company borders alleges the greatest demand for the IT to be successful.

  The problem is very crucial in India. India has 97% unorganized retail market.

  Unorganized business means that the demand and supply is made on an ad-hoc basis by each player of the supply chain thereby creating uncertainties in demand. Almost 50% of the fruits and vegetables produced in India are lost in the supply chain. In tonnage terms, this is almost the amount that is consumed in Great Britain (McKinsey report, 2003). However, systematic implementation of Information Technology to improve the inventory management can make a very big difference in the present time.

Maintaining the desired level of inventory is the most critical task before a retailer.The diversity of Indian customers, cultural variations and lack of distributional channels are responsible for rise in cost of inventory. Most of the retailers in India have inventory turns level in the range of 4-10% turns and stock out level between 5% and 10% as against the average inventory turns level of 18% and stock out level of less than 5% in US.Globally supply chains are fairly mature and efficient.This gives the retailer opportunity to improve profit margins without charging high price.

- **Ever increasing fuel prices**

  The frequent hike in fuel prices affect the price of retail goods since good transport is major factor in the pricing process.The wide geographical area of the country multiplier the effect of hikes in fuel prices.The organized retail is affected adversely because of this.

- **Lack of understanding**

  In India, the supply chain, is made up of the Supplier, Wholesaler, Distributor, Retailer and Consumer.The Supplier supplies the merchandise as per the orders received/ perceived.The Supplier also does the function of warehousing and dispatching of the finished products.Distributors provides distribution service by processing, executing the orders and providing after-sales services.Clearing and Forwarding Agents (C&F) perform all the distribution functions. Distributors also function like C&F agents, with the only exception that they raise their own invoice and collect the dues.

It is common that the supply chain is plagued with buffer inventories adding to the cost IT infrastructure has developed rapidly, and it has the potential to bring the agility and visibility in the supply chain by passing on the information quickly between different players. Strategic implementation of IT can improve (though not eliminate) the demand and supply imbalance.

- **Lack of supplier integration**

  In India, the retailers and suppliers operate distinctly without any integration.The retailers still are collecting information from their suppliers manually whereas in developed countries there is system of Vendor Managed Inventory. In this system, suppliers have access to the sales data of the retailers and thereby they plan automatic replenishments responding to the stocks available with the retailers. A Survey by KPMG confirmed that 100% retailers exchange such information manually.

✦ **Lack of vertical co-operation**

Contemporary retail business is chain oriented; therefore synchronization of demand and supply becomes a core question.The problems with the traditional vertical co-operation between organizations are manyfold. Instead of co-operating, actors dependent on each other have been seeking to achieve cost reductions or profit improvements at the expense of someone else in the supply chain. Companies engaging in transferring costs upstream or downstream arguably do not realize that such strategies will not make them more competitive, as all costs will ultimately make their way to the market in the form of increased end consumer prices.This understanding has to be developed which will take time.

✦ **The demand invisibility**

The demand invisibility, long lead time, poor synchronization of supply and demand, leads to the demand distortion. Supply chain in India is badly adapted to provide sufficient service even to the key segments of the product range.The other critical problem is that supply is discontinuous, even for some Fast Moving Consumer Goods (FMCG)! The increase in variability throughout the supply chain is partly a result of delays in information flow and miscalculating changes in consumer demand. The accumulation or draught of buffer stocks affects the order levels in each echelon, thus further delaying and distorting the information on changes in demand.

✦ **Supplier maturity and relations**

The problems from supplier side are many.The problem of on time delivery and in the required quantity is serious with Indian Suppliers. The services rendered by them are poor and need much improvement.The relationship between supplier and retailer also plays key role in this and Retailer finds regular supply a difficult task. Still suppliers are not mature and professional.

- **Availability of skilled manpower**

  This is a big problem before many sectors including retail. Retail sector is labour intensive and manpower with various skills are needed.In advanced countries such shortage is not witnessed and a large number of people are engaged in it e.g., in US 10-11% of the workforce is engaged in Retail whereas in India this share is between 7-8% only and that too is not fully equipped to meet the needs of the sector.There is a dearth of expertise in both at store level and managerial level.

- **Real estate costs**

  The cost of real estate in India is soaring high since last few years. It increases the fixed cost with small contribution per sale for retailers. Entry of retailers has further pushed the cost of real estate in metros and cities.

- **Low adoption and use of technology**

  Information Technology (IT) can help achieve great benefits in terms of the agility and visibility of the information flow. The problem is very crucial in India. India has 97% unorganized retail market. Unorganized business means that the demand and supply is made on an ad-hoc basis by each player of the supply chain thereby creating uncertainties in demand. Almost 50% of the fruits and vegetables produced in India are lost in the supply chain. In tonnage terms, this is almost the amount that is consumed in Great Britain (McKinsey report, 2003).

However, systematic implementation of Information Technology to improve the inventory management can make a very big difference in the present time Inspite of globalization and availability of high level technology in India, the Indian retailers are not tech savy as compared to their counterparts in advanced markets. The big retailers like Wal Mart are using Radio Frequency Identification (RFID)which helps in providing inventory visibility of higher magnitude and hence, makes the inventory management easy and efficient. As against this, the Indian retailers have not even completely adopted the bar code system.The technology is big challenge before the Indian retailers. Indian retailer with millions – or hundreds of millions "of transactions per period face significant technological difficulties in performing activity-based costing and other forms of profit analysis essential to understanding the details of what drives the business. to focus on continuous profits and performance improvement.

- **Lack of information**

  In India, the enterprises are helped more with information about input supply like finance, skills and technology and less, as compared,with information about output demand like new and existing customers needs.It is at this point of retail that a customer demand gets converted into a sale. By virtue of the location in the distribution chain, retailer is the most informed and qualified person to give information about the products.Retailer is very important for ensuring product availability and pre-call research and is also important for drawing up a good brand matrix.

- **Chaos in supply chain**

  The existence of chaos in a supply chain also means that it is impossible to make the right decisions for every player in a supply chain.The risk of making the wrong or ineffective decisions becomes the inevitable consequence and the supply chain is exposed to market risks. Thus, missing the market opportunities. a, supply chain cannot be responsive to changing market trends and customer preferences if the right market signals can not be obtained. Finally, market opportunities can be missed when customer orders with short order lead times can not be met.

- **Regulatory Provision**

  Indian economy despite liberalization and globalization is still under several controls and regulations.The retail sector is witnessing facing several problems from regulation side. A number of Acts and provisions obstruct the smooth functioning and operation of retailing.A number of provisions such as FDI restrictions, entry of foreign players, application of

Agricultural Produce Marketing Committee Act which presupposes that even small quantity purchases have to qualify like a wholesale deal, etc. are the challenges before retail sector.

- **Disparities in culture and taste:**

  This is perhaps the most critical factor since India is a country of diversity.There are differences in cultural preferences and tastes of people, festivals and ceremonies. There is no match with global culture. All these put a great challenge before a retailer since it requires inventory of various types of things.The MNCs face various problems and they have to come up with customized products.

- **Concerns over Indian retailers:**

  The organized sector faces stiff opposition from unorganized sector. Similarly foreign retailers are looked from suspicion. The smaller ones are scared that big retailer will capture their market share.There is another apprehension that the organized retailing will affect the general mass adversely. It will lead to unemployment to traditional retailers and will destroy the social fabric. There are about 15 million small shops serving the customers of the country.The Indian retail sector is required to take on challenges from global retail players such as Wal-Mart and Carrefour. Indian retailers have an advantage since unlike global retailers, they have a better understanding of the Indian consumer's psyche.Ultimately, a successful retailer is one who understands his customer.

- **Globalisation a challenge**

  Globalization of the market and India considering the opening of the Foreign Direct Investment (FDI) in the field of retail, has increased suppliers, manufacturers, brands, distribution and logistics partners. This has resulted in complex international supply network relationships. Mistrust and distorted information throughout the supply chain. This increasedlinks lead to higher costs and inefficiencies through over-ordering inventory and then ordering too little.

✦ **Psychology of Indian consumer**

The Indian customer is different from customer of advanced countries. He is looking for an emotional connection, a sense of belonging. Hence, to be successful any retail outlet has to be localised.The customer should feel that it is a part of his culture, his perceived values, and does not try to impose alien values or concepts on him. Indian customer is not keen to buy something just because it is sold by an international company. Ultimately, it depends upon the degree to which a global retailer goes for localisation and adapt Indian psyche.Other than tremendous size, global companies have nothing extra or special that the Indian retail business does not have.

* Indian Retailers today face various and complex challenges and barriers to success. they must compete globally and sell products locally, catering to the distinct and fast-changing tastes of local consumers while meeting competition that can come from global players. Retailers need to provide a differentiated shopping experience, while striving for growth and profitability. Adding to these many hurdles, operating in an environment of high transaction volume makes analyzing and reporting on crucial data a very challenging prospect

PROBLEMS

Challenges for retail and consumer product (R&C) companies are many in today's business environment as a confluence of market forces have created an extremely difficult climate. After all, most of the talent here is also on the move.That is the reason why India has slipped three notches down on the Retail Labour index.

Kalbag said, "The talent pool is shrinking and there is also a lack of good education institutes."India's peers, such as China and Brazil, took 10-15 years to raise the share of their organized retail sectors from 5% when they began, to 20% and 38% respectively. India too is moving towards growth and maturity in the retail sector at a fast pace. – Earnst & Young Report 2005.

"There is still significant opportunity, but the new players will have to deal with more competition, shrinking margins and more expensive real estate," said Hemant Kalbag of AT Kearney. It is also observed that regulatory and infrastructure issues have held back growth of the retail sector too.

FUTURE OF RETAILING

We live in exciting times. Only 3 per-cent of India's retail market is organised. The future shows tremendous potential for growth in the retail sector. Almost all large companies worldwide are looking to establish a base or stake in the Indian market.In this scenario, the Indian retail sector itself must seize the initiative to realise the dreams of contributing to a prosperous and booming economy.The focus should be on the Indian horizon before looking for retail opportunities in other countries because India itself is a big retail market.

In the near future, India will see a phenomenal growth of shopping malls and specialty retail stores.The specialty stores will cater for home, electronics, furniture, watches, sunglasses and assorted items.There will be more fashion stores for youth. Specialty retail stores and malls are the future of Indian retail market

* Till 2005 foreign businesses have only been allowed to operate franchises for fear they would harm indigenous firms but new regulations allowed foreign retailers to own 51% of outlets. **Foreign retailers will be able to own their own stores in India for the first time as part of a major government liberalisation of business.**

The Internet has given online retailers tremendous opportunities to collect data on customer behaviour and target people for different prices for the same merchandise. Website operators not only know what items customers put into their shopping baskets, but what items they remove before checking out. Retailers can monitor behaviour for long periods of time and figure out what web pages customers visit, which items they look at, and which products make particular customers happy. Online merchants also can tell if someone is a serious or casual shopper. Non-purchase visits to a site may tell the retailer as much about customers as those visits when they fill up their shopping carts.

The forecast for branded products was somewhat mixed.There is plenty of opportunity for goods and services that offer new consumer concepts or new product qualities, but most Indians believe brands are more expensive—even when they're not. It can be difficult for a new product to get over that initial hump with a customer, but it is estimated that the number of branded goods would grow from 2 per-cent to 20 percent of the consumer market over the next five years.

From a sector perspective, mall specialty stores that sell goods such as toys or watches should do well. "The consumer in India is far more aware than he ever was," It may take time for the shop "till you drop" mentality to take firm root in the cities and reach the country's more rural regions. But panelists agreed that the retail industry in India would continue to undergo significant growth and change in the years to come. For entrepreneurs looking to get in on the ground level, the industry offers a wealth of opportunity.

Earlier, consumers shopped at several stores; they are now shopping in a single store. Today, retail stores are sourcing from chain retail distribution centres rather than purchasing materials from different wholesalers. Further, retail chains are seeking exclusivity from suppliers. The growth drivers of organised retail in the country are growing consumerism, the Government stance to boost organised retail, and the availability of quality manpower, infrastructure and technology.

The growing consumerism in the country is a boon for retailers, Mr Vedamani said. "India will be among the top five economies in the world by 2025 and no marketer can afford to miss out on the India opportunity."

Modern retail would create up to 2 million direct jobs in the next two years. This growth would also offer local employment opportunities to millions of others. It would generate 'first-time' employment and 20 per cent of organised retail employees would become tax-payers in the country.

In addition, more than 50 per cent of the total employees in modern retail would be women.

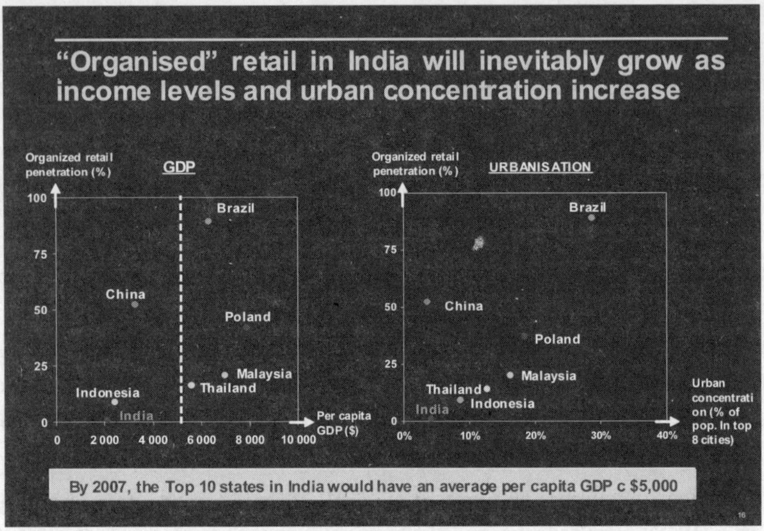

A note on Indian Retail sector- status and strategy

Indian retail sector was of the order of Rs.13,000 crs. In 2000 whereas it is estimated to reach at Rs. 50,000- 55,000 crs. During 2008-09, the size of different types of retail formats other than hyper market chains, Big Bazar, Malls, etc.has been quite large in India. Primarily, the formats are of 3 types – Haats, Melas, Mandis besides public distribution

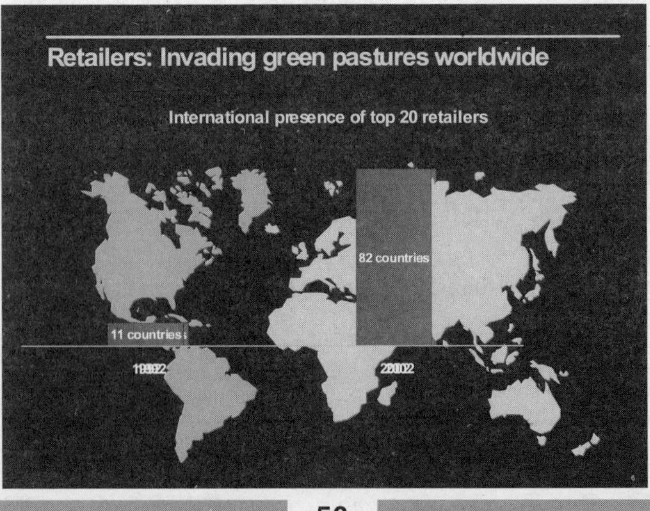

system, post office and mom- and - pop stores in the neighbourhood.A glance over the nature and size of these are given in the Table 1 given below –

Table I The different type of retail formats of India

Type of Retail	Features
Haats	Average sales per day Rs. 2.25 lakhsNumber of sales outlets per haat 300+No. of visitors per haat 4500 +Average sales per outlet Rs. 900Villages covered by per haat 20-50
Melas	Annually held : 25000 +Outlets held at every mela 800 +Average sales per mela Rs. 143 lakhs.
Mandis	Exists: 6800 average.Population catered to – 1.36 lakhs.

Source: BW Marketing Whitebook, ABP Private Ltd Calcutta, 2005, pp. 99-101.

A number of Indian and international professional organizations e.g., AT Kearney, Ernst & Young, PWC,Technopak, KPMG, ICICI, Synovate, Cushman & Wakefield, India Retail Forum and Images F &R, Research have observed that India is one of the best place for the retail growth. It has a number of advantages –

- About 89 million young population in various age groups below 45 years.
- Appx. 600 million effective buyers by the year 2010.
- Appx. 550 mn under the age of 20 years by 2015.
- Appx. 70 mn.Customers earning Rs. 8 lakh (appx.$ 18000) per year may rise to 140 mn. By 2011.
- In 2006, total consumer expenditure is Rs. 2,000,000 of which expenditure on retailing is likely to Rs. 55000 crs. By 2010 this may increase to Rs. 2 lakh crs.
- By the end of 2008 appx.100 mn.Sq.ft. of quality shopping space would be available..

- In the coming years space for 15000 new outlets, 100 hyper markets, 500 departmental stores, 2000 supermarkets, is likely to be available.

A number of large retailers have already entered on the stage and are planning to operate chain of stores in near future.The plans are given in the table II.

Table II Plans of Big retailers between 2010-2015

Sl.No.	Retailer	No. of stores	Floor Space	Investment Rs.Cr.
1	Reliance	—	—	30,000
2	RPG	500	4 mn. Sq.ft.	
3	Life style	-	-	450
4	Rahejas	55	-	-
5	Subhiksha	750	-	650
6	Pyramid	150	1.75 mn.sq.ft.	-
7	Trent	Existing = 27	1mn. Sq.ft.	-
8	More	220	-	300
9	Vishal Group	220	5 MN. SQ.FT.	1250
10	Bharti Group	100	-	31,500

Source: www.knightfrank.com/research reportdirphase 2./10949

A number of malls have already came up in different regions of the country. A brief idea can be gathered from the Table III.

Table III Regionwise Malls in India

S.No.	Location	No. of Malls	Built up area Mn.Sq.ft.
1.	North India	49	21.82
2.	West India	46	10.64
3	South India	28	6.66
4	East India	11	2.40
5	Total	134	41.52

Source: Knight Frank R;M Review Quarter 3,2006:

Development of malls in various cities of the country during 2006 can be seen from the Table IV

It is estimated that there are appx. 1.2 crs. Retail outlets in India of which two third are located in rural areas, however the organized retail outlets are still smaller in number and located in big cities only.

Table IV Malls in India City	Number of Malls		Area in mn. Sq.ft.	
	2005	2006	2005	2006
National capital region	14	18	3.35	6.67
Mumbai	7	14	2.45	4.60
Bangalore	5	1	1.06	0.5
Hyderabad	3	4	0.74	0.65
Kolkata	2	1	0.45	0.70
Pune	2	6	0.41	2.2
Lucknow	2	1	0.34	0.40
Indore	1	0	0.30	0.
Jaipur	1	1	0.20	0.25
Ludhiana	1	1	0.20	0.20
Cochin	0	2	0	0.85
Chandigarh	0	2	0	0.40
Chennai	1	2	0.40	0.65
Ahmedabad	0	1	0	0.65

Source: ICICI Property Services Research

The organized retail market has been of the size of appx. Rs. 35000 crs. Out of which largest share of about 40% is accounted for by textiles and clothing however there is fast growth in food and beverage sector, the share of which was 19% during 2005. The Table…V….. shows the size of various sectors both total and organized .

Table V Category wise market size, market share and penetration

Category	Total Retail Market		Organized Retail market		
	Estimated market Size in 2005 Rs.bn.	Market Share %	Market size Rs.bn.	Market Share%	Penetration %
Food, Beverage Tobacco	7738	75.8	65	19	1
Cloth & Textile	716	7.0	141	40	20
Consumer Durables	416	4.1	43	13	10
Jewalleries & Watches	416	4.1	25	7	6
Home Décor &Furnishing	300	2.9	25	7	8
Beauty care Products	214	2.1	7	2	3
Footwear	104	1.0	32	9	31
Books Music & gifts.	87	0.8	11	3	13
Total	9990	100.	349	-	-

Source: Alok Mehta,Shreyansh Mankad and Hema Bhatia – Retail – the Critical challenge, Welingkar Institute, Mumbai.

Barriers to Growth

The retail sector is growing very fast however there are a number of barriers the sector is witnessing in India. Some of the factors which are responsible for this phenomenon are give below-

✦ **Size and Structure of Retail Formats**-The Indian market is highly fragmented and the size of retail formats has wide variation.The range goes between 50 to 50,000 sq.ft.The traditional formats are still operating in their own style and the size is quite small.

Table VI Global Retailers entering in India

Rank	Company	Countryof origin
1	Wal- Mart	USA
2	Carrefour	France
3	Ahold	Netherlands
4	Metro Group	Germany
5	Kroger	USA
6	Tesco	UK
7	Target	USA
8	Rewe	Germany
9	Costai	USA
10	Aid	Germany

Source: M +M Planet Retail.

Changing Scenario and Strategy

Retailing is now a new buzzword in India and dynamic young people as well as blue chip companies take pride in calling themselves 'shopkeepers'. 'In India' according to various Census figures more than 5 lakh stores and shops are there besides many other retail business e.g., travelling salesman, temporary shops in fairs,TV shopping etc. The retail store employs 8 to 10% of working population and generate over Rs. 13.5 trillion of consumer spending and both of these two are increasing day by day.Currently, the Indian retail industry is valued at $330 billion of which organised retail is about nearly three per cent.

Rapid and Deep impact

The retail business can emerge within a few hours to 2 years. When a train or bus is held up for some reason near a village, many sellers emerge within an hour or so whereas a big company can plan to start a mall may take 12 to 24 months to start, through conceiving the idea, conducting feasibility studies, getting approval, arranging funds, developing infrastructure etc.In both the cases there is rapid and deep impact on its neighbourhood to the entire economy.The outlets opened by Indian Coffee House earlier and now the Subhiksha, Big bazaar etc.

have changed the life style of the people.The style of working of these retail stores change the process of supplies alongwith the consumer behavour.

For a successful retail store, it is necessary that it maintains consistent quality at all stores at various places to establish its credibility and brand name and has to develop a number of norms, standards, checks continuously. It has to develop and maintain the efficient distribution and logistic system which should ensure uninterrupted supply, economic inventory and avoid unnecessary movement of goods etc. to become efficient and cost effective

The retail market is peculiarly complex. A successful retailer must have not only the right products at the right place and the right time but also the right price. In addition, the number of products managed in retail is unusually high. A leading retail chain manages around 4,00,000 products.

An organized retail store generates higher level of skill employment opportunities in its stores and support functions such as operational management, buying, merchandising, information technology, logistics, etc. A retail store provides employment to 100-200 people directly and many times more indirectly. Moreover it is responsible for development of an area, its infrastructure, and many more services.Once the people start going to a mall the transport services, many petty sellers emerge, parking and many other services develop thereby the entire local area develops.Thus, it acts as growth engine.Thus, retailing has become a social and community activity.

India tops the list of 30 most attractive countries for mass merchant and food retailers looking to expand overseas as per an annual study of retail attractiveness among 30 emerging markets conducted by A.T. Kearney, a management consulting firm.India's retail market is vastly underserved and has grown by 10 per cent on an average over the past five years.The Kearney study adds that it is also one of the most fragmented retail markets in the world – the combined market share of the top five retailers totals less than two per cent. What drove India to such an attractive slot are the current moves to ease curbs on direct foreign ownership of retail outlets.

Thus global retailers such as Wal-Mart, Carrefour,Tesco and Casino, and others such as Marks & Spencer and the Benetton Group will all surely enter the Indian market. Pantaloon's Biyani observed "When we ventured into cities and towns like Sangli, Durgapur and Nasik, we were surprised to see the rising consumerism there, which made me believe that retail is not just an urban phenomenon." A difference between these shops and the larger retailers is that the family-owned businesses typically allow purchases on credit, so shopping there may be a necessity for liquidity-constrained shoppers who cannot obtain credit.

The retail boom in India is likely to push up the number of malls in the country but uncertainty remains about the success of these malls. According to industry experts, only 10-12 per cent of about 120 operational malls in India have been successful.These are numbers available with various retail and real estate analysts.There is also confusion regarding the definition of a mall in India and often departmental stores are erroneously referred to as malls. "There is a big void of skilled retail professionals who can manage these malls efficiently,"Nevertheless, there will be some losers in the retail game, but these are unlikely to be the mom-and-pop stores.A study from Mexico found that Mexican Wal-Marts and affiliated stores are predominantly targeted to consumers from the middle and upper classes, unlike in the United States where the target market is lower-income consumers. Indian scenario is not much different to it.

Inadequate planning, improper zoning, poor tenant mix and accessibility are major reasons behind the poor performance. A successful mall is where everyone (developers and retailers) is making money. Unfortunately in India, malls are seen as real estate ventures and people do not appreciate the service part involved in it.Important aspects such as design, tenant mix are being overlooked while developing a mall.These days whoever has some land plans to set up a mall.Only 25-30 per cent of the developers really go into the depth of understanding the retail business. A possible solution could be a revenue sharing model between the developers and retailers instead of fixed rentals.If developers and retailers agree to share their revenue, then both will work towards the success of the mall. However, very few are willing to accept this model because most developers do not have the experience and confidence that the malls will succeed.This is not only because of geographical, cultural and language diversities but lack of enterpreneurship.Though India is one country, from a business perspective it is divided by tax boundaries, administrative procedures, government policies and mindset of the people. Management of business becomes extremely complicated because of these factors.In some places, they even vary from city to city.This does not mean that nothing can be done to become successful.

It is very difficult to define a success mantra or model but if developers and retailers join hands at the planning stage and positive government policies are frmaed, then there is a strong possibility that the retail business will be a success.The natural question arises what should be the strategy for success in retailing.

'RETAIL STRATEGY':

A number of strategies have been adopted and suggested for success of retailing, such as–

Penetrating Pricing

"The phrase 'retail strategy' is usually an oxymoron, but not for big players like Wal-Mart. It's not really so much about marketing or pricing strategy.Instead, [the company] shrinks costs.In absence of proper analysis, it's easy for them to execute that strategy in the local market. When they go into a new market, they don't try to figure out how price sensitive the consumers are.They just charge prices slightly below market.That attracts customers to their stores.

Joint Venture

Sometimes buying existing retailers or working through joint ventures is the best strategy because retailers may be unable to ramp up fast growing enough otherwise."ompanies don't always feel the need for full-fledged control, so they find partner with local firms.The U.K.,for example, has a very different marketplace density than the U.S. and real estate is much more expensive. So a strategy based on acquisitions or joint ventures makes sense.

Build to order

No matter how a firm enters a new market, there are at least two ways it can play the retail game once it has established itself, says Fisher. "One approach is customer knowledge – to know your buyers inside and out.The other is product concept – doing something unique."1 Fisher cites McDonald's and Swedish furniture giant IKEA as examples of concept-driven firms."IKEA isn't so much about knowing the customer as it is being an expert in product category positioning,"he notes.

IKEA had an operational strategy and executed it well from country to country.Part of it is that virtually everything is drop-shipped to stores. So there was no reason they couldn't similarly drop-ship here. Furniture was an industry where, with most retailers, you ordered something and then waited 12 weeks to get it. It's still mostly a build-to-order type of business. IKEA cut down that time by pushing delivery and assembly onto the customer.

Knowing the customer

The number and nature of customer are critical factors in retail business.In China, for instance,Wal-Mart sees a huge opportunity considering that the living standards are high enough in the urban areas. Every body is expecting that China continuing to grow at a fast rate. The U.S.'s per capita GDP may be higher, but China's population is obviously much bigger.How far a concept-driven enterprise can go is anyone's guess.The question is whether Wal-Mart's distinctive elements – the everyday low price, the people greeters, etc. – can trump the need for deep customer knowledge in each country. Is their supply chain and cost reduction strategy enough?"

There are two things retailers need to do. One is to adapt to the local competitive environment.The second is cultural.In the current economic and geopolitical climate, it's hard to say how reactions may change. "U.S. firms benefit from their 'Americanness' sometimes.But it's a double-edged sword. At the same time that 'American'is an attraction – it can cause problems, too."Edward B.Shils,emeritus professor of entrepreneurial studies at Wharton, agrees that geopolitical and social factors are not static."Firms can enter any country as long as they are sensitive to cultural differences and how they change over time depending on world affairs.Employing locals to manage the operations there can help, but the companies should be aware of the economic, sociological and cultural milieu in which they are operating."

Sometimes retailers don't do well because of stagnant or nonexistent consumer interest. As reported in *Home Channel News*, Home Depot did not meet expectations in Chile or Argentina, but it has done quite well in Canada. One explanation for this is that Canadian consumers were already exposed to the brand and hands-on culture of their U.S. neighbours to the south.

Do it yourself

In the U.S.,"the do-it-yourself ethic was already quite strong. Home Depot provided a large assortment at good prices in what had been a regional, scattered environment. It put a lot of lumberyards out of business. In other countries, where labor is often cheap, the do-it-yourself mentality was not quite as developed.Home Depot is still struggling, for instance, in Mexico. When there isn't a lot of disposable income, someone might barely be able to buy six concrete blocks and a bag of cement."

Carrefour, which was the first international retailer to establish a presence in Asia, has also been successful in many countries but did not fare well in the U.S. "Carrefour didn't stay on strategy. It wasn't clear what they were trying to do. Carrefour probably didn't succeed in the U.S.because people saw the hypermarket as a bit of a European anachronism.In US, there's no compelling reason to buy a refrigerator and the food to put in it in the same store.

Few Considerations:

Thus it is difficult to prescribe any model which may lead to guaranteed success.To become successful in retailing it requires to–

(a) Take a holistic approach to retail development, combining theory and practical ideas to cover the entire scope of what it takes to succeed in retail.

(b) Combine core personal and company values with the business expertise to create a meaningful brand.

(c) *Craft a retail presence to develop customer loyalty*

(d) *Identify the best retail locations;*

(e) *Build a management team, organization, and systems - whether there are 1 store*

(f) *Innovate and renew the brand. –*

(g) *"Instead of profit the motivation should be the passion* to drive for excellence or stay with the concept during the hard early years and become unique."Being profitable is necessary but not sufficient. The retailers ensure that they have a profitable model. but profit cannot be the primary mission. It's a different universe of thought entirely. A company focused primarily on profits likely will fail to focus on creating and sustaining unique core values that make it different and therefore more competitive.

(h) Use technology for faster inventory infill.The price/value retailers continue

(i) To improve quality and hold down prices, which is forcing the middle and upper tiers of retailing to improve quality as well as remain differentiated.

(j) Inner city neighbourhoods represent one of the best opportunities for companies looking to increase retail sales.Inner-city stores provide jobs to local residents within their community. The jobs give people hope and the operating stores are more convenient and improve the aesthetics of the neighbourhood which encourages others to invest locally.The higher standard of living created by more employment encourages increased spending and thus more retailing opportunities. here are other positive changes, some subtle but important. Instead of people having to spend over an hour commuting on public transportation to get to work, they can spend more time closer to home helping their children with their homework or being active within their community.

(k) Delegate management powers to line people.Companies need to distinguish when top managers need to be in charge versus when they need to empower their employees to make decisions. Airlines need to have central decision making over things such as flight schedules and security. But they need to empower people to make decisions when they can make life easier for customers. When customers arrive at an airline counter, they often have unique travel needs.They are under a lot of stress. Travellers need to get someplace on time, and they are tired.They are relying on the transportation network. Companies that are involved with one-to-one contact should train people to make positive decisions for customers in such situations whenever possible.This is exactly what most private airways are doing to win customer loyalty. You feel you are talking to a human being, not a robot.

(l) Develop balancing capability. While bringing out a new brand or a new concept an entrepreneur has to be able to coldly assess why his or her idea is solid enough, different enough, new enough to be able to grab market share from existing enterprises. It needs to balance the enthusiasm one needs for a new brand with the cold assessment one needs to really know if the brand will have legs? Balancing enthusiasm and reality is one of the hardest things for a retailer to do.The emotional response is a very powerful driver. When one gets excited about something he is doing, his ego is reinforced. One step is to develop a solid strategic plan with rational go/no-go decision points. Another is to do a great job analyzing the financials.

(m) Obtain the opinion of mentors and outside experts that can bring back to reality. From thebeginning, one should design a program about whom to talk to, when to talk to them, and what kind of feedback you're looking for. It's important to find someone who will be brutally frank. Some people are so kind they don't want to spoil ones enthusiasm, or they don't want to diminish the drive, so they won't be honest.one should seek honest feedback– a difficult and complex task.

(n) A adopt appropriate strategy to win the hearts and inds of consumers and create "disciples of the brand".Successful marketing positively presents product attributes by tying it to lifestyle, function and the needs of the consumer. It's not "spin" if one is telling the truth. Sometimes, the same company uses the same approach to marketing over and over again, or many companies use the same approach, so the repetition may make something feel like propaganda. To the extent that any one marketing vehicle overwhelms the consumer, the message may feel like propaganda. It's up to companies to constantly seek fresh vehicles.

(o) A adopt "hub and spoke" strategy as a good way to pursue rapid but sustainable expansion into new regions: Dominate an area, then move outward from there. Entrepreneurs will definitely benefit from understanding the military approach to things. Military planners constantly do what-if analysis, do backup plans. They constantly think about what would happen if this or that attack went badly. Their mindset is to constantly move forward, to keep the other guy retreating.That preparation, that constant state of alert, that desire to always be moving — all these have many parallels in business.

(p) Be careful not to get too focused on the competition. One remembers when Lotus would introduce three new spreadsheet features and Microsoft would retaliate with five new features, and suddenly we had 20 new features that nobody could figure out how to use? Two competitors got so focused on each other that they forgot to do something the customer needed. Responding strictly to what the competitor is doing can also lead to what we call the "99-cent burger wars," where everyone converges on the same features and the only differentiation is price.That's a losing strategy.So many analogies exist between business and the military in planning and tactics, but there are differences too.

(q) Become customer oriented. In Indian condition the issues relating to language, customs, religion, taste habits and locality make much difference and strategy has to be tailored to suit to the needs of customers.The strategy adopted by McDonald is a good example, nevertheless it took a long period to adapt itself to the local flavour.

(r) Take care of the four 'rights' – the right product in the right place at the right time and at the right price – and they really are failing miserably." Fisher estimated the costs associated with mismatches between supply and demand, for example, as "about 10% of revenue, in an industry where profit is about 2% to 3% ..."Today we have powerful information systems that can store customer data in giant warehouses. Some companies keep data for a few weeks, others for a number of years. In both cases, however, many businesses don't know how to use the information they collect and often don't make it available to their merchants. The result is that customers are still going away dissatisfied because what they want isn't in stock?Turning customer data into action is eminently doable and very effective.

(s) To improving capabilities in certain basic areas:

- **Accurate Forecasting:** Rather than relying on the gut feel of a few individuals, companies should update forecasts based on early sales data, track and estimate forecast accuracy, test products and implement a blend of bottom-up and top-down forecasting. Example: Book and music retailer Borders tracks sales by product category at each store, and periodically uses its merchandise planning system to automatically adjust each store's assortment. A store in Alaska, for instance, might be well stocked with books about small planes.

- **Supply Chain Speed:** Companies should improve supply chain responsiveness so as to reduce stockouts on hot sellers (popular items that sell out) and also to reduce markdowns because less merchandise needs to be ordered initially. Example: Zara, which ships apparel worldwide from Spain, stores raw materials and reserves production capacity at factories in anticipation of demand.

• **Risk-Based Inventory Planning:** Companies should track stockouts, use this tracking to estimate lost sales and inventory levels to balance the risks of lost sales and excess inventory. Example: At Bulgari, the Rome-headquartered jewellery manufacturer, the researchers found that stockouts on a single item had lowered company profits by 5% of sales.

* **Understanding the customer:** Customers in different countries are different from each other, and the retailer must make detailed study to understand them. Not only demographic but socio-psycho factors require deep understanding.

Strategy for India

India is overcoming tradition and poverty to create opportunities for retailers ready to take a chance on a new playing field. Rising incomes, increased advertising, and a jump in the number of women working in the country's urban centers have made goods more attainable and enticing to a larger portion of the population. At the same time, trade liberalization and more sophisticated manufacturing techniques create goods that are less expensiave and higher quality

While deciding to implement a new technology, major factors considered are scalability and user adaptability. This is because the most important thing in retail business is customer friendliness.Ultimately, the business is all about providing service to the end customer.The customer in the store is the *prima facie* reason why a retail business opts for a particular technology. A perfect business model for retail is still in evolutionary stage. Procurement is very vital cog in the retail wheel. The retailer has to fight issues like fragmented sourcing, unpredictable availability, unsorted food provisions and daily fluctuating prices as against consumer expectations of round-the-year steady prices, sorted and cleaned food and fresh stock at all times. It is difficult to a suggest one single strategy for Indian market however there are some guidelines available.

Kishore Biyani had launched the country's first ready-made trouser brand in 1987 and diversified from there. Now, as CEO and managing director of Pantaloon Retail (India) Limited, he oversees thirty-two department stores in fifteen cities. But success doesn't arrive overnight. Biyani cited a few factors to consider when launching a retail operation in India:

- ✦ Foreign investment is restricted.
- ✦ India's culture favors saving, not spending.
- ✦ Real estate costs are high.
- ✦ The taxation and legislation system is complex and difficult to navigate However, there are many more issues which need attention in Indian retail business since the western model does not work in India for several reasons.

  (a) There exists a vast majority of small shop keepers numbering more than 50 lakhs spread over throughout the country who are afraid of with the big retailers and oppose them.

  (b) There is opposition from NGOs. Some economists and social reformers too.

  (c) The illiterate public will not be comfortable with big stores and malls.

  (d) The supply chain is not efficient particularly at remote places and small towns.

  (e) The poor prefer to buy on credit rather than in cash.

  (f) Consumer research has shown that at least for now, Indians are unlikely to make a purchase at a mall that involves spending over $250. Intergold's stand-alone stores have low walk-in traffic, but customers are more likely to make a purchase in the $400 and up range.

  (g) "Weather is an issue particularly in the monsoon season that makes shopping indoors an attractive prospect.

  (h) A number of studies found that forecast for branded products was somewhat mixed. There is plenty of opportunity for goods and services that offer new consumer concepts or new product qualities, but most Indians believe brands are more expensive—even when they're not. It can be difficult for a new product to get over that initial hump with a customer, but some estimated that the number of branded goods would grow from 2 per-cent to 20 per-cent of the consumer market over the next five years.

The Conclusion

While there are no easy answers, the success of some of the big players on the global stage does suggest that it's not impossible to export a good strategy elsewhere. Historically if we observe we note that every decade sees a retailer who innovates so powerfully that it rewrites the rules for other retailers and for all companies in the retail supply chain." In the '80s it was Wal-Mart. In the '90s,it was Amazon.com and now In India it is Pantaloon and Reliance Fresh. We believe the next retail innovator will be the one that best combines access to consumer transaction data with the ability to turn that information into action." "Retail is a slippery slope. The margins are often not high, so you save an extra rupee here and there. Most succumb to that temptation." So far, players like Wal-Mart, Costco, and Home Depot are staying the course.They stick close to what they do well.In India, there is severe opposition from local Kirana merchants, some political parties and others who do not subscribe the philosophy of organized retailing. It is imperative that a flexible model is evolved that captures the value chain and allows retailer to evolve with the customer and existing retail shopkeepers and middlemen.

Reference

1. *Arthur Rubinfeld,* Built for Growth: Expanding Your Business Around the Corner or Across the Globe, *published by Wharton School Publishing 2003.*
2. Marsh*all Fishe*r Professor Wharton operations professor and two co-authors professor Ananth Raman of the Harvard Business School and Anna Sheen Mc Clelland, a former research associate at Wharton "Rocket Science Retailing Is

Almost Here – Are You Ready?" in the July-August 2000 issue of the *Harvard Business Review.*

Questions:

1. "Organised retail still is infancy in India." Discuss.
2. Discuss the historical development in retailing in India.
3. Discuss the global environment for retail sector.
4. Keeping in mind the developments happening on the Indian retail scene, what is the need of the hour for Indian retailers?
5. "India has reached the growth stage in retail Discuss."
6. What is the strategy that needs to be adopted by the retailers to ensure that they succeed?
7. What are the opportunities and challenges before retail sector in India?
8. What changes you will like to suggest for development of retail in India?
9. What future you see for the retailing in India?
10. "It is apprehension that small kirana store will die with the growth of organized retailing." Comment.

CHAPTER 3 Types of Retailing: Retail Models And Theories

TYPES OF RETAILING

Retailing is one of the oldest business and with the time it has been undergoing changes in nature, content and operations.

RETAIL TYPES

There are three major types of retailing. The first is the market, a physical location where buyers and sellers converge. Usually, this is done in town squares, sidewalks or designated streets and may involve the construction of temporary structures (market stalls).

The second form is shop or store trading. Some shops use counter-service, where goods are out of reach of buyers, and must be obtained from the seller.This type of retail is common for small expensive items (e.g. jewellry) and controlled items like medicine and liquor. Self-service, where goods may be handled and examined prior to purchase, has become more common since the 20th century.

A third form of retail is virtual retail, where products are ordered via mail, telephone or online without having been examined physically but instead in a catalog, on television or on a website.Sometimes, this kind of retailing replicates existing retail types such as online shops or virtual marketplaces such as Amazon.[3]

Retail organisation can be buyer or merchandiser led. Shoppers Stop is a merchandiser led organisation, whereas pantaloon is a buyer led organisation.

As has already been explained retails functions are Merchandising, Buying, Store Operations, New Store Operations, Human Resource, Finance, Supply Chain, Marketing Research, Logistics and Design.Two most important retail functions are Merchandising Buying and Store Operations. The types of retailing is influenced by the need and emphasis given on these functions. Store organisations can be centralised or decentralised. In Shopper's Stop for example, 90% of the merchandise is same, only 10% is different, they have similar stores. Store operations are mainly administrative in nature, they have little choice on product selection, they have very strong MIS.On the other hand, Pantaloon is decentralised. Here, buying, merchandise is done at the store level, but it increases the cost.

Store operations can be front office interaction with customer, floor management etc. Back office include house keeping, Security, liaisoning, Maintenance and Cash office (Cash grab is done 2 to 3 times a day). There are different types of retailers depending on their size, shape, product lines, amount of service they offer and prices they charge etc. The classification may be based on following:

- Store based retailing
- Non store retailing
- Service Retailing

Store Based Retailing- This can be of two types–

(a) Form of Ownership
(b) Merchandise offered
(c) Pricing.

Ownership– This is the critical decision every retailer has to make, i.e., what should be the structure of the organization.This has long term implications and a number of factors needs to be considered while making this decision–

- His vision regarding the nature and size of present and future business.
- The degree of control which he wishes to have.
- The legal and regulatory provisions and issues relating to it in future.
- The implications of each type of structure.
- Tax provisions of various structures.
- Availability of finance and other resources.
- Specific problems and issues related to a locality/region/ country.

Independent store – When one owns and operates individually a retail store. He may seek support of his family members or friends without giving them ownership rights.The sole proprietorship continues from generation to generation.It can be small or large, typical example is mom-and-pop stores.The person owns all the assets and profits and also bears the liability. In India the examples are, Benzer, Premsons, Amarsons, etc.

ADVANTAGES:

- ✦ The decisions are quick.
- ✦ It is the simplest and least expensive structure.
- ✦ Good customer relations.
- ✦ High service levels.
- ✦ Can be closed at the will of the individual.
- ✦ Strategic clarity.

DISADVANTAGES

- ✦ The lack economy of scale.
- ✦ No best management.
- ✦ Cannot advertise more.
- ✦ Limited resources.
- ✦ Unlimited liability.

Independent store– This is another pattern which is also found commonly in India is partnership.In this two or more, but limited persons can share ownership the responsibility and profit are shared between partners on pre agreed basis.

ADVANTAGES:

- ✦ Pooling of resources.
- ✦ Benefit of complementary skills.
- ✦ Relatively easy structure.

DISADVANTAGES

- ✦ Unlimited liability.
- ✦ Possibility of conflict
- ✦ Delay in decision making

Independent store– Corporate chain stores operate multiple stores. In this type of structure two or more outlets are under a common ownership.There is similarity in the merchandise offered to the customer in these stores.Wal-Mart, Sears, Wills Sports, Van Heusen, Arrow, Globus, Shopper's Stop, Food World, etc. are some examples of the chain retailer.

ADVANTAGES:

- Advantages and economies of scale
- Better bargaining position *vis a vis* suppliers
- Improve inventory management
- Better personnel
- Improved customer service
- Better prices to customer
- Networking facility
- Cost effectiveness in advertisement, sales promotion, etc.

DISADVANTAGES:

- Slow in responding to environment
- Difficulty in satisfying specific customers of a locality
- Poor customer relations may happen
- Problems of managing big organization

Franchising – A Franchise is a contractual agreement between two parties where the one is franchiser and the other is franchisee.It is a contractual association, between a manufacturer, wholesaler, or service organization and independent business people who buy the right to own and operate one or more units in the franchise system.The Franchisee conduct business under an established name in return for a fee or compensation.The franchise may be for a single store or a multiple number of stores or a for a region or country. Louis Philippe, Arrow are examples of individual franchises in India whereas Mc.Donald's operation at a level of two regional franchise.The franchise receives all profits from the operation of the business after paying the royalty/fee to the franchisor.

This is a great motivation to him to push up sales.The franchising may be for the product or trade mark in which the products are sold on the name of franchiser.

Franchise are mid way between chain and independent stores.The franchiser provides use of brand, product, advertisement support, specifies store, training and sometime minimum guarantee also. Franchisee provides space, administer space, buy stocks or take on consignment. Good location and caliber of the franchisee decides the success of the agreement.

ADVANTAGES:

- Enhanced image.
- Advantage of expertise to all units.
- Branding is possible.
- No resource constraint.
- Economy and cost effectiveness from the suppliers side.
- In case of business format franchise, inventory control and management is better.

DISADVANTAGE

- Lack of variety from customer's viewpoint.
- Customer relationship may become impersonal in certain cases.
- Curtailment of freedom in decision making to an individual store operator.

Leased Departments – A leased department consists of space in a large retail store that is rented to an outside vendor.These are also termed as shop-in-shop. It is a good method available to the retailer for expanding his product offering to the customers.One can find jewellery, shoe and perfume sold in this method in large departmental stores.In India larger retail chains are setting up smaller retail outlets or counters in high traffic areas like malls, departmental stores, multiplexes and other public places like airports and railway stations.

ADVANTAGES:

- ✦ Advantage of greater expertise within the store.
- ✦ Providing additional products and services to customer which may not be related to the Store.
- ✦ Reduction of cost to lessee.

DISADVANTAGES:

Branding and image building of the products sold at counter may be affected adversely.

Consumer Co-operatives– When few persons together forms a co-operative body to run a store that may be called Consumer Cooperative.This type of store may be small or quite large like other cooperative bodies. It serves its members as well as others but the basic objective is to provide customer satisfaction to its members A large number of Sahkari Bazaar is found in India in various cities.One gets products at a reasonable price since the profit is not the only objective of such stores.Members of the cooperative hold shares and some member may be active in running the store while others may be passive.

ADVANTAGES:

- ✦ Reasonable price and assurance of quality product.
- ✦ Customer satisfaction is the major objective.
- ✦ Convenience of the member customers is important.
- ✦ Expertise of members can be availed in running the business.

DISADVANTAGE:

- ✦ The members may not have the experience and skills or running a store.
- ✦ The growth is doubtful.
- ✦ Incase it becomes too large and run by hired executives, it becomes a corporate body and the interest of members may not be assured since profit motive may become the major goal.

II- Classification based on Merchandise offered.

Stores which are classified on the basis of the merchandise mix that they offer. Broadly they may be classified in two categories-

- **General Merchandise store**
- **Food oriented store.**

General Merchandise store– These stores offer various products to the customers and try to satisfy their customers in one store itself. This has been a powerful retail institution. Here, a number of types are found:

Departmental Store: A retail organization that carries a wide varieties of product lines–typically clothing, home furnishings and household goods; each line is operated as a separate department managed by specialist buyers or merchandisers.These are the large retailers that carry a wide variety of products.They are termed Departmental because they are organized by departments such as electronic goods, sports, men's wear etc.Each department acts as a independent mini store–having allotted space, personnel and managers.The first such store was started in Paris in 1838.

In general, a departmental store is a big retail outlet serving to customers. Mostly these stores become the anchors of major shopping centres. Now it is popular in most of the countries In India Shopper's Stop, Globus, Lifestyle, Benzer are some of the example of such store. In India the size of an average department store varies from 20,000 to 40,000 sq. ft. and stocks anywhere between 50,000 to 1 lakh SKU's (stock keeping units).

ADVANTAGES:

- Mostly they are having standard store design.
- The lay out is designed which makes shopping easier for customers.
- They offer new customer services, e.g., restrooms, reading rooms, restaurants.
- They are able to undertake research in area of consumer information.
- To attract more customers they become more innovative.

DISADVANTAGES:

Innovations,research etc.increase the cost which has to be recovered from the customers.Competition among departmental stores become intense and sometimes harmful.

Food Retailers

Food being most important item of daily consumption, food retailing assumed significance.As the mass merchandising industry began to mature, food retailing has been focused as a vehicle of growth.Special courses in food retailing have been introduced in Universities. A variety of food products are made available.The specialty stores in food products are also available.

SPECIALTY STORES

A store that carries a narrow product line with a deep assortment with in that line. Such stores keep one or a few limited products only. A store specializing in a particular type of merchandise or single product of durable goods or a range of normally complementary durable goods

product categories is known as specialty store. In such mode customers are able to get high level of service or information about the product. Such stores concentrate on jewellery, fabrics, sport goods, furniture, etc. In India such stores are emerging fast.The Gap, Ikea High & Mighty, Big and Tall, Proline fitness station are some of the examples of specialty.

ADVANTAGES

- Customers get high level of service including detailed information about the products.
- More variety and quality products may be available in such stores.

DISADVANTAGE

- Customer has to move from one to other store for satisfying his needs.
- The Total amount of sales may be less thereby increasing the fixed cost.

Convenience Store– As the name indicates these are the stores which are located in areas which is convenient to the customers.Not only location but their timings, availability of type of products, etc. are also organized keeping in mind of the needs of customers.They offer a limited line of convenience products, like bread, milk, grocery, etc.In fact our local kirana or bania shop (known as mom and pop store) is a good example of convenience stores. Such stores target the customers of surrounding area who want to make their purchase immediately.

Super Market– Super Market ***"a retail market that sells foods, convenience goods, and household merchandise arranged in open mass display."*** *It is l*arge, low-cost, low-margin, high-volume, self service store that carries a wide variety of food, laundry and household products. The word **"supermarket"** means different things to different countries around the world, as global supermarket chains have discovered recently. However, it is certainly a fact that supermarkets began in the U.S. Such markets are controlling more than 30% of the grocery market in many countries. From the beginnings of the retail trade there has been a trend for general stores to increase in size and for specialist stores to combine (so called "combination stores"). It is believed that store chains have existed from as early as 2,200 years ago; the first self-service store was first introduced in 1916 in the U.S. So, all the elements of the supermarket were in place. In the absence of a universal definition for the supermarket there can be no authoritative reference point in history that marks the shift from small general stores to supermarkets. There are, however, important milestones, such as the growth of The Great Atlantic & Pacific Tea Company, which, in 1910 opened the Economy Store format, selling basic dry groceries such as tea, coffee and tinned foods.These items were sold in relatively high volume at low margin, another hallmark of the supermarket.There is no standardization on the parameters to distinguish super markets with other department stores, in India, it is one of the fastest growing retail formats in the country.Foodworld Subhiksha, Food Bazar are some of the examples of super markets.

One of the criticisms against the supermarkets and big chain stores is related to their impact on the town. As they expand, they destroy the community feeling, the exclusive charm of small towns. It has also beenobserved that chain stores adopt several anti competitive practices as colluding with suppliers.

Although sometimes super stores are helpful also since they attract people who earlier did not enter a small shop before because there was no shop nearby. These stores are responsible for popularising the habit of shopping.

The next two milestone were the introduction of faster means of transport, especially the motor vehicle, and the rapid take-up of home refrigerators. These two elements allowed more affluent consumers to require larger quantities of food in one shopping trip. As this one-stop-shop tendency spread throughout the U.S., shopkeeper and store chains became increasingly aware of the critical need to attract these customers to their stores. This resulted in the lower prices, but also drove these companies to try new ideas such as the Drive-In store. As these stores were specifically for car users, they did not need to be situated in the expensive centre of town but instead were typically found in lower rent neighbourhoods on the outskirts.

III - PRICING BASED

Discount Stores– A retail institution that sells standard merchandise at lower margins and selling at higher volume.Virtually they are a type of department stores.The difference may be in service and merchandising These stores generally, offer limited customer services and charge lesser price than departmental stores.The products may also differ in the quality, fashion,etc.in these stores. Discounters can be EDLP (Everyday Low Price) or discounters

They create an image of large volume, low cost products. Wal Mart is a good example of Discount store.The main focus in these stores is on value consciousness.In reality, such discount stores came on the scene during recessionary period but now continued across all situations and at all income levels.Such stores have grabbed the market of departmental stores in a big way.

Factory Outlets– The manufacturer himself opens a retail shop in certain areas and sell at a lower price to the customers.Factory outlets do not contain A grade merchandise, they provide 20-30% discount.

India is the only country where factory outlets are franchised.

Off price Retailing– Off-price retailing operation that is owned and operated by a manufacturer and manufacturers' surplus, discontinued, or irregular goods are sold. Here, the products are sold at less than retail prices.Either such retailers buy manufacturer's seconds, overruns and off seasons at a deep discount and sale them. Such products may be old sizes, unpopular colours, fashion or with minor defects. When they are owned by the manufacturer lit may be called factory outlets,. Such stores are intended to dispose off the stock and to increase the business. The format largely depends on volume sales to make money.

Category killers– It is a specialty retailer which offers a very large selection in the chosen product category at an economical prices.They focus on one category having deep stock.They buy and sell cheap and dominate the category.Sometimes they are called power retailers.They carry some of the same merchandise but are downsized to give the customer a smaller more intimate store.The price charged is normally lower than big stores.Nalli's in Chennai may be termed as a category killer in sarees.

Price clubs (cash and carry)

They are also known as Warehouse clubs and Stores.Such stores are developed to satisfy such customers who want low prices every day and willing to give up service needs.In price clubs one has to pay a membership fee.These store keep limited assortment of goods.Their size may be large also.They rely on fast moving, high turnover merchandise. Many such clubs do not keep perishable items since they want to avoid storage cost.

Hypermarket

The word hypermarket is derived from the French word hypermarche, which is a combination of a supermarket land a department store. Hypermarket is a combination of EDLP and discounters.They are now synonymous with one stop shopping.The cheapest prices will normally be found in these stores. Such; markets are usually part of a retail park, along with other shops, restaurants, petrol pumps etc. Other facilities such as banks, ATM, photo processing shops etc.are also provided.The hypermarkets are designed to attract customers from a significantly large area with their low price offers, unique range and other offers.Mostly the prices are discounted.Hypermarkets in each metropolitan city in India targeting price conscious consumers, providing mind boggling assortment of products is the trend of the future. Increase in labour force and variability in demand and human resource requirements helped in promoting these formats.

Mall

Mall is not a store: it is enclosed, organised managed market space.Every mall has an anchor, which is a famous store which draws crowd to the mall. Multiplexes are not necessarily anchors as people who watch movies normally shop less. Malls are managed in the sense that only best stores are kept and worst stores are removedFrom kiosks *to large anchor stores*, a mall has many retailers competing with each other under one roof. There are generally 3 to 5 anchor stores, or large chain stores, and then dozens of smaller retail shops. Typically the rent in a mall location is much higher than other retail locations. This is due to the high amount of customer traffic a mall generates. Before selecting this type of store location, be sure the shopper demographic matches the description of your customers. Mall retailers will have to make some sacrifices in independence and adhere to a set of rules supplied by mall management.

Shopping Center

Strip malls and other attached, adjoining retail locations will also have guidelines or rules for how they prefer their tenants to do business. These rules are probably more lenient than a mall, but make sure you can live with them before signing a lease. Your community probably has many shopping centers in various sizes. Some shopping centers may have as few as 3 units or as many as 20 stores.The types of retailers,and the goods or services they offer, in the strip mall will also vary.One area to investigate before choosing this type of store location is parking. Smaller shopping centers and strip malls may have a limited parking area for your customers.

Downtown Area

Like the mall, this type of store location may be another premium choice. However, there may be more freedom and fewer rules for the business owner.Many communities are hard at work to revitalize their downtown areas and retailers can greatly benefit from this effort. However, the lack of parking is generally a big issue for downtown retailers.You''ll find many older, well-established specialty stores in a downtown area.This type of store seems to thrive in the downtown setting.

Free Standing Locations

This type of retail location is basically any stand-alone building.It can be tucked away in a neighborhood location or right off a busy highway. Depending on the landlord, there are generally no restrictions on how a retailer should operate his business. It will probably have ample parking and the cost per square foot will be reasonable.The price for all that freedom may be traffic. Unlike the attached retail locations where customers may wander in because they were shopping nearby, the retailer of a free standing location has to work at marketing to get the customer inside.

Office Building

The business park or office building may be another option for a retailer, especially when they cater to other businesses.Tenants share maintenance costs and the image of the building is usually upscale and professional.

Home-based

More and more retail businesses are getting a start at home. Some may eventually move to a commercial store location, while many remain in the business owner's spare room.This type of location is an inexpensive option, but growth may be limited. It is harder to separate business and personal life in this setup and the retailer may run into problems if there isn't a different address and/or phone number for the business.

Non Store Retailing

The most simple form of retailing is direct selling to consumer.It is non store retailing.The basis of such selling is the direct relationship with the consumer. Such retailing may be classified broadly as-

Direct selling

It involves direct personal contact with the consumer by visiting at his home or place of work A large number of products e.g., cosmetics, food, home appliances, etc.are being sold in this manner. Although Pheriwalas were common in India since long, however in organized form this has been became popular in mid 90s. It is interesting to note that nearly 70% of sales people are women.

Direct response marketing

In this process, the customer is made aware of the products/ services offered through a non-personal medium like mail.Catalogues, phone, television or the internet.

Catalogue retailing – Eliminates personal selling and store operations. Here, the key is use of customer database to develop targeted catalogs that appeal to narrow target markets.It is convenient to both the seller as well as customer.

Television shopping- With the growth of television in India, marketing has been done through this. The product is advertised giving details about the product features, price and other things on television. Phone number to contact of major cities are shown on the screen. Buyer can place the order by calling, and the product is delivered at home.

Others

There are some other types of retailing also which have emerged during last few years.

Automated Vending

The use of technology has provided this facility when the products are available to the customer round the clock and the person is not required to supply at the counter. Some routine products are made available through these machines where putting the specified coin will deliver the product. Earlier weighing machines on railway platform and

now banks ATM centres are the most successful example of this format in India.It avoids the recurring cost of labour.

The Cash and Carry

This is a wholesale format that helps small retailers and businessmen.The customers do their own order picking, pay in cash and carry the merchandise with them.It offers a wide assortment of goods thereby saving the time of the customer.The cash is some times replaced by a member card Metro is one of the largest distributor of food products world wide including India,Airport Retailing

Airports in many cities of the world serve as mini shopping plazas for the traveler. Airports are focusing on retail to convert airports into exciting, retail/entertainment centre along with travel.

Service Retailing

It involves the retail of various services to the consumer.Retail banking, car rentals, service contracts are the examples of service retailing.The success largely depends upon differentiation, innovation, business process reengineering, micro planning, marketing, intelligent pricing, customization, technological upgradation, promptness, cost reduction, etc.

Some shops sell **second-hand** goods.In other cases, especially in the case of a **non-profit** shop, the public donates goods to the shop to be sold. In **give-away shops** goods can be taken for free.

There are also"consignment"shops, which are where a person can place an item in a store, and if it sells the person gives the shop owner a percentage of the sale rice.The advantage of selling an item this way is that the established shop gives the item exposure to more potential buyers.

Concept Store – describes a store which is identified by a special mix of brands and products.It"s a modern experience of shopping, always in motion and highly innovative. The store addresses particular groups of customers: e.g. luxury, design, streetwear-customers. They"ll find (all) the products, they identify with in one store. A typical mix of products and brands in a concept store would be: fashion, shoes, (home) accessories, books/cd"s, cosmetics, food, toys, hardware for daily use.

The range is wide and some stores even change themselves and the products regularly, to stay flexible and surprising.

A Concept Store is a mixture of a department store and a boutique

Tuangou; loosely translated as **team buying** or **(group buying)** is a recently developed shopping strategy originating in the People''s Republic of China. Several people – sometimes friends, but possibly strangers connected over the internet – agree to approach a vendor of a specific product in order to haggle with the proprietor as a group in order to get discounts.The entire group agrees to purchase the same item.The shoppers benefit by paying less, and the business benefits by selling multiple items at once.

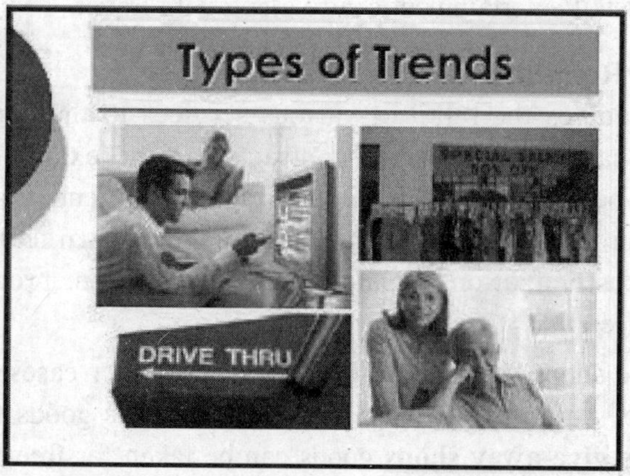

Door-to-Door Retailing

This kind of retailing is as old as retailing itself and is still very common, although less so in recent times. A door-to-door salesperson may be self-employed or employed by a company and will usually specialize in a particular product group, often household items. Although it is common for them to visit houses, they may also sell to businesses.

Area of Coverage

Door-to-door salespeople can be split into two main groups.The first group are those that stay in one locality, selling to regular customers. Greengrocery or fresh meat sales are typically made by these local salespeople. They will have regular "rounds" and will try to time their visit so that they appear at a given location at the same time each week (or day or month). This way, customers may come to depend on them. The local door-to-door salesperson may also try to extend their round to take in more customers.

The second group are traveling salespeople.They may procure goods in a more opportunist way, taking advantage of a bargain when it comes along, or buying goods to coincide with environmental changes or particular events in the calendar. For instance, such a salesperson may sell warm clothes at the onset of cold weather but also sell gifts at festive times. Once they have sold their goods, or reached the point where they have few customers left to sell to, they will move to another area and repeat the process. As well as buying goods to sell on, they may also sell goods that they have made themselves or that their family or community have made. They also may provide services to customers, such as mending, sewing, light maintenance, knife sharpening etc.

ADVANTAGES

One advantage of being a door-to-door salesperson is that the overheads are relatively low. Some door-to-door salespeople will carry all of their stock on a vehicle but others may store it in their homes or a small warehouse (sometimes known as a "lock up").They can also be flexible in the range that they can carry.This can allow them to be very up-to-date with the products that they can offer.

DISADVANTAGES

Disadvantages include the lack of security in travelling door-to-door whilst carrying a high value of stock or money (some door-to-door salespeople can take card payments, thus reducing the risk of carrying a lot of money). Another disadvantage is that where a shop's customers come to the shop, door-to-door salespeople spend a lot of valuable time and often transport costs visiting their customers – and there is no guarantee of a sale.

In brief the store formats are summarized as under – Store formats are of four types: independent, chain stores, franchise, and concession of shop in shop. Independent store are one or two in number, can be small or large, typical example is mom-and-pop stores. Advantages are quick, v. good customer relations, high service levels. Disadvantages are the lack economy of scale, no best management, and cannot advertise more.

- Chain stores are 3+,advantages are economy,best management and can go for advertisement.
- Franchise are mid way between chain and independent stores. The franchiser provides use of brand, product, advertisement support, specifies store, training and sometime minimum guarantee also. Franchisee provides space, administer space, buy stocks or take on consignment. Good location and caliber of the franchisee decides the success of the agreement.
- On the basis of products stores can be department, mass merchandiser or specialty stores.
- Department stores are multi-brand, multi-department stores
- Mass merchandisers are multi-department stores, they also carry their own labels.
- Specialty stores can be single line, e.g,. apparels, limited lines, eg., men's apparels or super specialty stores, e.g., formal shirts .
- Stores can also be divided in the basis of pricing, they can be factory outlets, discounters, Category killers, price clubs (cash and carry) or catalogue retailers like IKEA.
- Factory outlets do not contain A grade merchandise, they provide 20-30% discount. India is the only country where factory outlets are franchised.
- In price club, you have to pay a membership fee.
- Discounters can be EDLP (Everyday Low Price)or discounters.
- Hypermarket is a combination of EDLP and discounters.
- Mall is not a store: it is enclosed, organised managed market space

- ✦ Every mall has an anchor, which is a famous store which draws crowd to the mall. Multiplexes are not necessarily anchors as people who watch movies normally shop less.
- ✦ Malls are managed in the sense that only best stores are kept and worst stores are removed.
- ✦ Retail organisation can be buyer or merchandiser led. Shopper's stop is a merchaniser led organisation, whereas pantaloon is a buyer led organisation.
- ✦ Retails functions are Merchandising, Buying, Store Operations, New Store Operations, HR, Finance, Supply Chain, Marketing Research, Logistics and Design.
- ✦ Two most important retail functions are Merchandising Buying and Store Operations Store organisations can be centralised or decentralised. In Shopper's Stop for example, 90% of the merchandise is same, only 10% is different, they have similar Stores.Store operations are mainly administrative in nature, they have little choice on product selection, they have very strong MIS. On the other hand Pantaloon is decentralised. Here buying, merchandise is done at the store level,but it increases the cost.

  Store operations can be front office-integration with customer, floor management etc.Back office include house keeping, Security, liasioning, Maintenance and Cash office (Cash grab is done 2 to 3 times a day)

RETAIL THEORY:

Retail theory deals with

(a) how the retail development took place and whetherany general principles can be drawn on this basis,

(b) how do businesses interpret the rules and make decisions about retail location and typology?

One of the important things about the context of the original theories is that they were developed for understanding traditional models of retail, and have been interpreted for new formats and conditions.Some subtleties of the theories have been lost; for example, that utility can be measured by square feet of space-while perhaps a good indicator of the quantity of available products, it is still a proxy to estimate the utility of the visit. Likewise, the term "agglomeration" was used to describe groups of stores operating in proximity, not the square or linear feet of shelf space of a single retailer.The theories of retail gravitation do not suggest that the old models of retail do not work, or are outdated. Rather, they describe how the demographic shift in population to lower density regions and the highway and super-highway infrastructure shape the modern retail landscape, and hint at the preconditions for making retail succeed in urban environments.

There are many different aspects to the current practice of market assessment, and different interests will look at the question from different perspectives and use analytic tools to answer the questions they are concerned with.The overview a developer will examine is the "Area Demand" which quantifies demand through employment, population estimates, demographic in, which formation, income and retail sales. Retailers increasingly use "Consumer Demand" analysis that qualifies the type of demand through market segmentation,"psychographic" profiles, and local consumer buying preferences. "Market Share" analysis evaluates the existing competition, and "Trade Area Analysis" helps in location selection to optimize market share.In short, such analysis determines what to build and where to build it.

The theories developed in the 1930s of central place /agglomeration and gravitation are still the basis of thought for retail theory.The big ideas can be summarized as follows:

(a) Central Place Theory

The theory explains the size, number, and spacing of distribution centers to serve a dispersed population A model that ranks communities according to the assortment of goods and services available in each area. At the bottom of the hierarchy are communities that represent the smallest central places (centers of commerce).The central place provides the basic necessities of life. Further up the hierarchy are the larger central places, which carry all goods and services found in lower-order central places plus more specialized ones that are not necessary.

Retailer will develop the format where it is most convenient to large population and cater to the needs of hinterland. The market concept has been developed on this basis itself. Retailers seem to have had an idea that the centers should be like "self sustaining" villages; small cities in and of themselves, with a mix of housing and business They took the logical steps in determining the size of the centers based on populations. It seems that they had a ideal in mind- that of the neighborhood main street, with neighborhoods that supported local shops.

(b) Retail Gravitation Theory

People will travel the shortest distance possible to, for example, buy a cup of tea. At the same time, larger concentrations of services that provide choice and utility will attract customers from larger distances. You might go a little bit further to get a cup of specialty tea at a place that also sold your favourite magazine.Understanding the balance of distance and utility of a trip, the retailer can estimate the likelihood of how many people will be drawn the extra distance to buy both a specialty tea and a magazine, rather than the instant tea available more conveniently. This is the generalized logic of increasing grocery store sizes to capture shoppers from a larger trade radius, and is the basis of "Gravity Models" to predict the ability of larger stores to "out-draw" the competition.

In 1931, William Reilly at the University of Texas in Austin hypothesized a law of retail gravitation (that was restated by Curtis Publishing Corporation in 1947 as follows):

M=D/1+sqrt(P1/P2)

This equation determines (estimates, really, but more on that in a second) the point of indifference between a customer going to one location versus another based on the population of each center and the distance between them and the customer.This law establishes a relationship between the utility of size versus distance to a location. A later version of this theory in 1963 by David Huff framed the relationship in terms of probability, laying the ground for estimating market capture. The framework of all of this analysis underscores the importance of the two previously mentioned factors: utility (of agglomeration, and with it choice of products), and time.

Although it is commonly referred to as a law, Reilly's hypothesis has been verified with only moderate degrees of accuracy, suggesting the principle is sound, but the exact relationship varies by location, and may have other factors (perhaps qualitative elements) that are not accounted for. Also, Reilly determined the "size" not by the square feet of retail space, or the variety and aggregation of services offered,but by the local population, that was used as a proxy presumably since at the time in 1931 retail was still concentrated in population centers.

Reilly's Law of Retail Gravitation attempts to quantify the relative value of agglomeration.This articulates the utility of a site that offers greater benefits for the customer for the distance traveled.When a customer can satisfy many needs with one trip, even if the trip is longer, they will make the trip because the "utility" of the experience is perceived to be higher.This is the strategy pursued by a regional mall that includes a wide variety of shops as well as food and entertainment in order to increase the perceived benefit to the consumer for the sunk cost of the trip. Another example of this utility is when the quality, type of goods, or pricing is simply unavailable elsewhere, thus making the perceived value of the goods or experience more important than the cost of getting there. An example of this is a high-quality restaurant that may be located in an out-of-the-way place but still attracts customers from miles away. Similarly, Wal-Mart made it's way establishing stores in rural places where people were under-retailed and were accustomed to driving many miles to shop. By providing a wide selection at discounted prices, (promoting a perception of utility) it was able to draw rural customers from large distances.

One interpretation of retail gravitation is that it encourages retailers to build the largest facilities possible to "out draw" competition.Where densities are lower, larger boxes are required to draw a sufficient market from a larger area. (Look at the Walmart model to better understand how a big, juicy retail magnate on a rural highway can draw from many distant rural communities with low enough densities that do not support competing local services.)This logic, as a response to servicing low density areas, has caused new suburban retail to rely on size as its primary competitiveness and creates a culture of "category killers" where retailers either dominate a market or go out of business.

At the same time, there is a hierarchy of types of retail, based on the frequency of customer use, and the time cost of the trip.Some very basic questions differentiate types of retail markets: how many people need what is being sold, how often do they need it, and how far do they have to go to get it? People need groceries often, while appliances are needed only once in a very long time (depending on how reliable the machine is, of course).Stores with goods that require lots of visits annually are called "high-frequency" uses; others, such as appliance stores have fewer visits and are considered "low-frequency"uses.As the frequency goes down, typically, there are fewer shops.Consequently, there are more grocery stores than appliance stores for a given market, and people are willing to travel farther to go places with greater choice for appliances.It should not be surprising then, that "category killers" tend to best work with low frequency uses, where customers are willing to infrequently travel farther for better selection and price, allowing very large stores to service very large geographic areas.

This frequency hierarchy is another aspect of value versus time as described by Reilly and Huff.The shop with the highest perceived utility for the amount of time spent getting it will out-compete other locations. We have seen above how this has played out with category killers in low frequency uses.For very high frequency shopping trips, however, this means the closest or the most convenient shop to the consumer is likely to gain the sales—this is the retail strategy of convenience markets, where price of goods is a secondary consideration.This also means that urban shops, with easy access to the city residents, are still positioned to be the closest and most convenient retail services.

These theories elaborate the governing laws that show how retail locates as close to it's market as possible and in agglomeration of sufficient size to provide the perception of utility to the customer.They also help explain why the demographic shift in population to lower density regions and the highway and super-highway infrastructure shape the modern retail landscape.

This theory has been developed by the Community Builders Council in 1947 in U.S.Actually, they were struggling with making suburban shopping centers work and the idea has become a theory of retail. They were interested in building villages and communities.

However, rather than building villages and communities of people, the transportation infrastructure created the basis for support of the retail typologies we see in suburbs today.Roads affect retail formats in two important ways: street configuration and market access.

There is a relationship between the speed of traffic and the nature of development on the street.While the causation is a bit like the chicken and the egg, the relationship is quite clear.Fast traffic begets buildings with large setbacks and large separations.Locating buildings close together and close to the street tends to calm traffic.In fact, building to building distance and street width is more significant than street width alone in reducing traffic speed. Roads networks also determine the access a retail business has to its market.In suburban highway conditions this is measured in vehicle counts, which is really a proxy for understanding the number of people or households in the trade area for whom location has easy access and visibility.In the suburbs where travel speeds are higher, supporting low density housing, the effective area served by a retail store is greater, and as we have seen with the ideas of retail gravitation, stores are increasingly encouraged to be as large as possible to capture as much of the local and regional market as it can.It is common to justify the success of the resulting big boxes and discount retailers by their sales, despite public opposition to their business model or architecture. However, these "actions of the general public", supporting the stores with their residence, should not be read as a universal economic superiority or necessity of the format, but evidence of its appropriateness to the surrounding suburban conditions.Where smaller scale road networks provide local access with slower speeds to more populated areas and many people walk or use public transportation, access to such a wide geography is not necessary and smaller formats are still efficient. This is because of the other implication of retail concentration: that proximity to markets is a balance against shear size.Consequently, different retail formats are best suited to different road networks and population distributions.This theory is nearer to gravitational theory.

THEORIES OF RETAILING DEVELOPMENT.

Retailing developed , primarily from two considerations one, making money by acting as middlemen between producer and consumer and other the needs and comforts of customers in the changing world.The socio economic and technological development. contributed in determining the nature and developing various forms of retailing.Nevertheless we can also analyse the development from theoretical perspective.Nevertheless we must keep in mind that no single theory is universally applicable.

A number of theories have been developed to explain the process of retail development.These theories are based upon the considerations of following phenomenon.

(a) Competitive pressures and their importance,
(b) Investments in organizational capabilities,
(c) Creation of sustainable competitive advantage,
(d) Implementation of strategic planning,
(e) Needs of the customer and his attitude.

These theories can be classified as –

(1) **Customer Expectations** –What are the needs of the customer?
- (a) Central Place Theory
- (b) Gravitational Theory
- (c) Community building theory.

(2) **Environmental** –The change in the environment in which the retailer operates results in change in retailing.
- (a) Environmental Theory.

(3) **Cyclical** – Where a particular pattern and phases are identified in the changes and the similar pattern is observed in related issues.
- ✦ Wheel of Retailing Theory
- ✦ Accordion Theory

(4) **Evolution Theory** – Where a new format is developed by the retailers as a result of intense competition or conflict between two types of retailers.***(Nicholas Alexander = International Retailing, p. 110)***

- Dialectic Process Theory
- Natural Selection Theory

ENVIRONMENTAL THEORY

The environment in which retailers operate is crucial in developing the process of retailing.The environment consists of social, economic, technology, cultural factors in which the customers, competitors and the retailer has to operate.The environment forces a retailer to evolve and change the strategy since it affects the sales, profitability and image.The environment may affect any single retailer or a group or all of them.A retailer has to adjust his operational behaviour with the changes in environment.

The growth or decline, success or failure, profit or loss largely depends upon the environment.The size, nature, type, timing, location, etc. are influenced by the environment which may change at any time. The retailers have to adjust and bring suitable changes in accordance with the environmental changes.The success of a retailer depends upon how quickly and sometimes in anticipation, desired strategy is formulated to face the challenges brought through changing environment.Those who either do not adapt to change or adapt with delay face setback and failure. The retailers are supposed to observe keenly the environment and react immediately to gain in the market.The promptness pay.

CYCLICAL THEORY

The Wheel of Retailing

A well-known established theory of retail evolution is "The Wheel of Retailing" propounded by ***McNair ("M. P. McNair, - Significant trends and developments in the post war period" 1958.)*** According to this theory, the retail innovators often first appear as low price operators with a low cost structure and low profit margin requirements, offering some real advantages, such as specific merchandise.This enables them to take customers away from more established competitors.The theory suggests that a retailer witnesses 3 phases in a cyclical manner.

A retailer enters in the market and start prospering and developing its business.This is made possible by adopting strategies which costs to them, e.g., offering a greater range or acquiring more expensive facilities. In this process he loses the focus that was so important to him when he entered the market.This type of 'trading up' occurs when the retailer becomes established.This provides opportunity other competitors to enter and adopt the process.The new entrant offers more discounts and new services with lower cost structures.Thus the existing retailer becomes vulnerable and looses the market share.Thus he moves to next place along the wheel.Scrambled merchandising occurs as the retailer adds goods and services that are unrelated to each other and the firm's original business so as to increase overall sales and profit margins.Ultimately the retailer faces the problem of top heavy and declining return on investment.The entire process is termed as the "wheel of retailing".

(S.Brown, Varioation on la Marketing Engime"- Journal of Marketing Management, Vol. 7, 1991). This theory can be explained from the example of departmental stores, which entered on the scene as a low cost competitors to the small retailers, gradually they developed and became prosperous,then the supermarkets and discount stores entered and departmental stores suffered a lot.Thus, they reached to the third phase of wheel.

Retail Accordion theory

This theory suggests that retailer initially enters a market as a generalretailer, gradually with experience he focuses on particular group.To grow they tend to diversify their business.

It suggests that retail institutions go from outlets with wide assortments to specialized narrow line store merchants and then back again to the more general wide assortment institution.It is also referred to as the general-specific-general theory.

Hollander ***(Hollandler.S.C.Whjeel of Retailing,Journal of Marketing, Vol.48 (No.3) ,1960)*** observed keenly the evolution of retail and he used the analogy of an orchestra comprised exclusively of accordion players to describe the dynamically shifting retail structure. He explained how general stores moved to specialise. Soon they widened their range of merchandise and added as new classes of products. Hollander states that the retailers have two options before than.Either thy have'open accordions'- representing general retailers with broad product ranges or'closed accordions',indicating a narrowing of the range, focusing on specific merchandise.He notes that at any point of time, any one type of retailer would outnumber the other. However the situation would continually change through the entry and exits of different stores.Then ultimately the successful retailers would face the same phases as explained in the "Theory of Wheel".Hollanders considers that this analogy explains the complexity of the retail scene land the way in which different attitudes towards successful retailing would come in and go out of fashion at different times.This may be termed as "Accordion Theory".The process is cyclical and can be explained through the ***figure*** ....

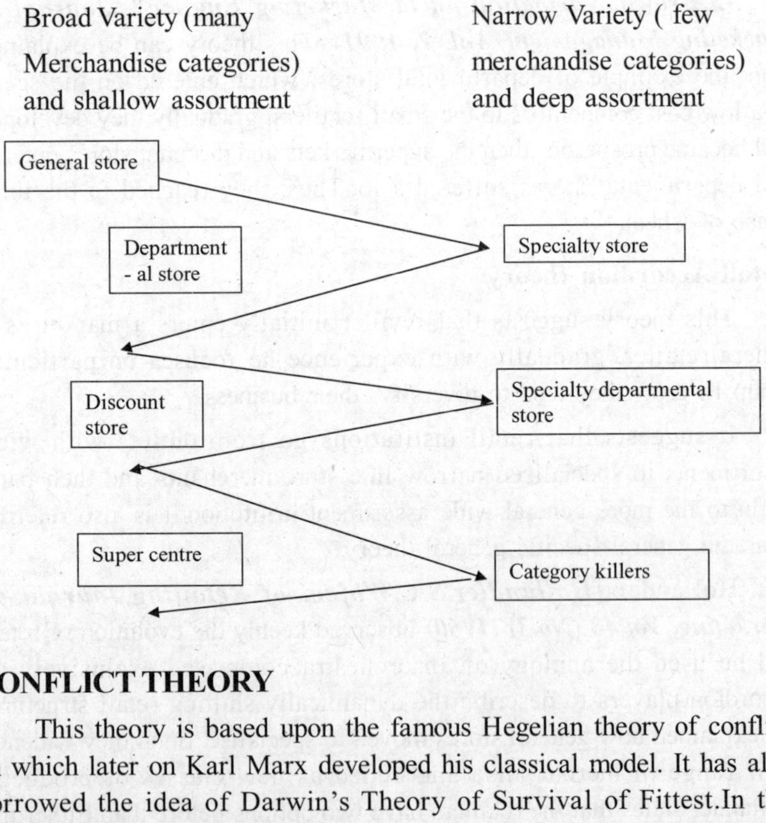

CONFLICT THEORY

This theory is based upon the famous Hegelian theory of conflict on which later on Karl Marx developed his classical model. It has also borrowed the idea of Darwin's Theory of Survival of Fittest.In the context of retailing, conflict arises because of competition and in this process that organization will survive and grow which is fittest. Conflict may creep up among similar formats or within broad retail categories. Incase of retail, it is observed that innovation does not necessarily results in reduction in the number of formats rather it leads to emergence of a new format. In practice the competition takes place among most of the formats which encourages increase in number of total formats in the market.The consumer may be benefited by this but conflict arises among retail formats.Retailing thus evolves through a dialectic process by blending of two opposites to create a new format, the process which was mentioned by Hegel in the context of ideas and theory.

The application of the said conflict theory is having slight variation in case of retailing. The process may be like this-

(a) **Thesis** –The first position such as there may be an individual retailer as corner shops at many places and might be doing quite well.

(b) **Antithesis** – Over a period of time an improved version opposed to corner shops may emerge, e.g., the departmental stores.This is antithesis and a challenge to the thesis, i.e., corner shop.

(c) **Synthesis**– A blending of the thesis and antithesis may come up and a new format may emerge.The conflict between corner shop and departmental store results in emergence of a new concept, i.e., super markets.Thus, place.

This theory assumes existence of conflict as a natural phenomenon and continuous possibility of growth and development of formats.

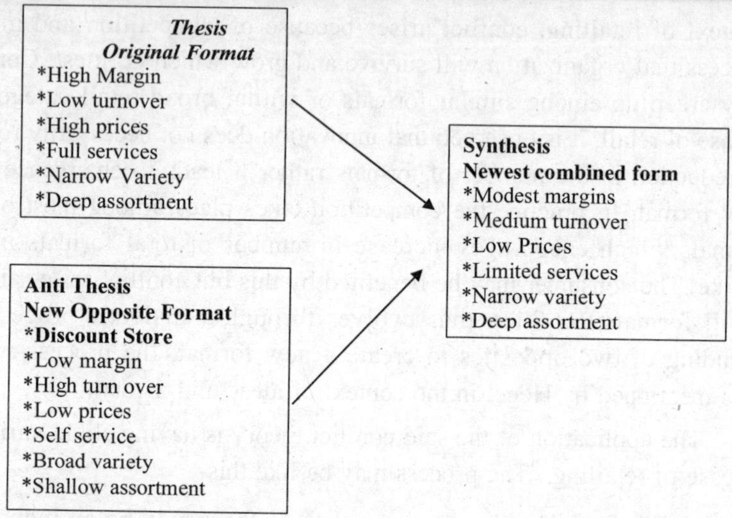

OTHER THEORIES

Retail life cycle

A theory of retail competition that states that retailing institutions, like the products they distribute, pass through an identifiable cycle.This cycle can be partitioned into four distinct stages: (1) innovation,(2) accelerated development, (3) maturity, and (4) decline. Philip Kotler *(Marketing Management, P.Kotler, Millennium edition p.303)* has explained the concept of product life cycle and since retailing is similar to that, the same theory can be applied here.

The Retail life cycle theory explains the process of changes through time the retail outlets developed. A glance at the historical development suggests that retailing shows an "S shaped" development curve.here are four main stages in the life cycle of retail.

(1) Innovation

A new type of organization emerges with the objective of improving the satisfaction to the customer and other advantages.It differs in a big way from the existing retailers. It requires innovation. In this stage, new concepts are introduced where the number of competitors are limited.

The growth is fast in this period and the profitability is moderate.The duration of this stage may last from 6 months to 5 years.This will depend upon the nature of organization and degree of innovation.

(2) Accelerated Growth

The innovation leads to stage of growth and development. The investment level is high and the profitability too is high.There are a number of competitors now but the organization which has adopted innovation has an edge over others.It occupies the leadership and the growth is accelerated in a big way.

(3) Maturity

This is third stage when the organization is growing but started realizing the pressure from competitors.Some new trends are emerging and even new forms of retailing may come on the stage. Sooner the organization reaches at its peak and thereafter starts declining.Very soon the competition becomes intense and the number of competitors also increases resulting into the slowing down the growth.This also results in lowering down the profit.In case organization has a capacity to develop new strategy, it can maintain its position otherwise normally the slow down process starts creeping gradually.

Decline

Ultimately the retail organization starts lagging behind the other new emerging companies and the decline starts.The rate of growth not only slows down but may turn negative.The profitability also declines and the costs particularly overheads increase in a big way.The organization needs to assess its situation and take proper decision.

This life cycle is similar to that of any other organization and business.The duration and nature of the stage may vary from organization to organization but more or less all organizations face these stages.The retail life cycle stages and the profitability is depicted in the figure-

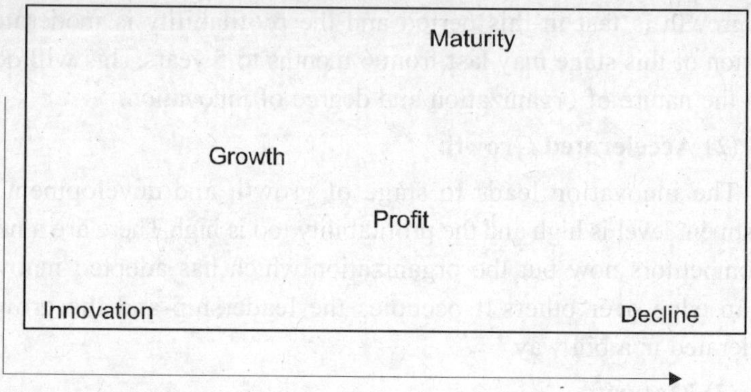

Innovation in retail

The innovation in retail is steadily taking shape in India.The process is such that it has the potential to change the way in which we purchase even the basic necessities such as groceries and vegetables.Innovation is happening not just at the backend, but also at the customer facing end. It's taking place all over, right from where the customer enters a store to the point where he leaves.This essentially covers the whole process of buying of products, right from selecting to decision making and paying at the checkout counter.

"Innovations in the retail industry are multi pronged and are aimed at enhancing the end user experience, optimizing resources and logistics, creating a technology platform to keep pace with the dynamics of the industry and manage the unprecedented growth given the geographic spread and diversity,"said Dr.Anurag Shrivastava,Vice President, Consulting Division, Wipro. Some of the key innovations include:

Customer identification using RFID:This involves identifying customers by issuing them smart cards embedded with smart chips. These cards would be RFID enabled and would give information regarding the customer like his preferences, shopping behaviour etc.

E-Catalog based selling: Here a limited range of merchandise is available in-store, while the range of a hyper format is made available through self browse kiosks.

Mobile Point of Sale (POS):This would enable the purchase of goods while putting them in a shopping cart.The customer would be spared the hassle of standing in long queues.

Digital Signage: Static signboards have not proved beneficial in terms of helping a customer track a product. Digital signboards integrated with an automated tracking system can make this easier.

Intelligent database: A detailed database of the customer is made available online and helps the retailer understand a particular customer's buying characteristics.

In addition, retailers are even deploying applications such as CRM for loyalty programs and personalized service and ERP, inventory management, supply chain management and security solutions, POS, master data repository, data management etc to get the basic infrastructure in place.

Large scale IT adoption is not equal across categories in the retail industry. There are eight key segments in the retail sector, food/ grocery/ vegetables, garments, electronics/electrical, cosmetics/medicines, home furnishing and furniture, lifestyle products (jewellery, shoes, watches), office products and multi product outlets.Lifestyle and apparels are more open towards IT.Even grocers are thinking of deploying basicIT solutions. On a whole every retailer is looking at a tailor made solution which meets his needs.

Where are we placed?

Retailers adopting IT innovations in India are still at an introductory phase, and in the process of understanding the benefits of IT in retail.

It is indeed the beginning.The market is showing trends which are difficult to predict.The Indian consumption pattern is changing.Thereby the needs of the retailer will evolve methods that will have to catch up to the pace of the need.That will drive innovation in adaptation.

Large and medium size retailers are going through the cycle of putting a robust transaction system in place which includes a suitable POS system, merchandise management system and a CRM system. Following this investment will be made in world class supply chain and logistics management system and business intelligence and analytics systems.

However, the innovation and deployment that is taking place in India is confined to the organized sector, which is a small proportion of the overall retail industry. Also organized retail in India is comparatively new, as compared to the West where it has been since the last 50 years.

The life cycle concept is also applied to various retail formats gradually emerged in retail sector over the years. Various forms of formats emerged and then grew faster and ultimately faced the declining situation over the years.

Retailer Scope – The Virtuous Circle

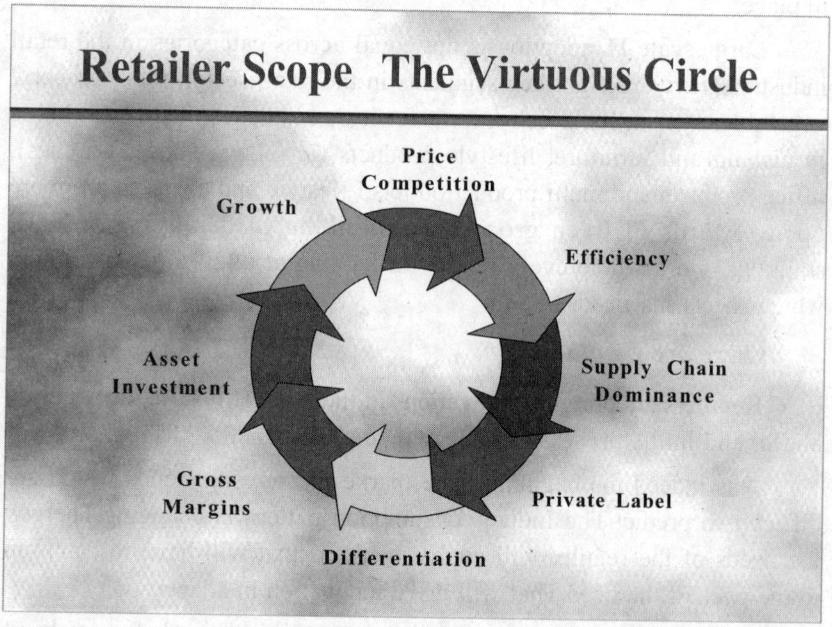

The Retail Revolution Consequences of the Nature of Change

The Retail Revolution
Consequences of the Nature of Change

1. Growth of Chains	➢ Increased buying Power ➢ Focus on Price as competitive weapon
2. Large Formats	➢ Decline in number of small stores ➢ Shift to Out of Town ➢ Exclusive Sites
3. Integrated and Dedicated Distribution	➢ The Application of I.T ➢ Control of Retail Stores ➢ Speed and Frequency of Replenishment ➢ Decline of Wholesalig
4. Retail Brands	➢ Differentiation by Format and Location ➢ Private Label ➢ Loyalty Programmes

RETAIL MODELS

CUSTOMER BEHAVIOUR

The business of retail is getting tougher every year.Consumers have more choice than ever and are far more selective about where they shop. With more retailers and more stores chasing an aging and discerning customer, it's no wonder that big names in retail have recently gone bust.From Merry-Go-Round and eToys to Service Merchandise and Woolworth,the retail landscape is littered with the bodies of fall an champions.Once shining stars of business, these former market leaders went from the top of the heap to the trash heap before they even knew what hit them.

A model of consumer's choice between different supermarket formats may help retailer to develop successful format.A number of formats may be considered, conventional supermarkets characterized by high-low pricing, wide assortment and some service,discount stores characterized by every-day-low-pricing, narrow assortment and no service, and hypermarkets,characterized by a pricing policy somewhat in between the two other formats, large assortment and some service.

Fundamental retailing lets customers tell retailers what they want through their actions in stores

- Simple analysis of KPIs (key performance indicators)will enable retailers to quickly identify and resolve basic problems and inefficiencies in their strategy and execution.
- Fundamental retailing enables easy access to the best and most appropriate information for all members of the retail team, enhancing the actions they take day in and day out Information sharing.

The approach also turns suppliers and customers into partners in retailers'success by sharing information that will increase their confidence in the business and encourage their active participation in its improvement.

The New Fundamental Retail Model

- **BASIC RETAILING** is the core function of the retail organization and includes such activities as merchandising, promotion, and pricing.
- **NETWORK** refers to the operational support required to execute the retail business process.
- **FULL CYCLE** encompasses the collaborative aspects of the retail business process.

BASIC RETAILING

The New Fundamental Retail Model:
BASIC RETAILING

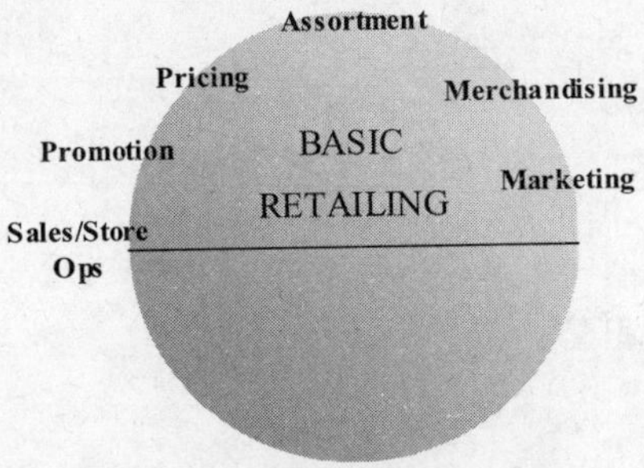

INTEGRATION CHALLENGES

- Timely knowledge of customer behavior
- Impact of promotional activity
- Price adjustments
- Overstock, stock outs
- Need for rapid analytics

INFORMATION FLOW

- Bi-directional flow of data between functions
- Rapid dissemination of data from checkout line to functions
- KPI and analytics Exchange of information with Network and Full Cycle

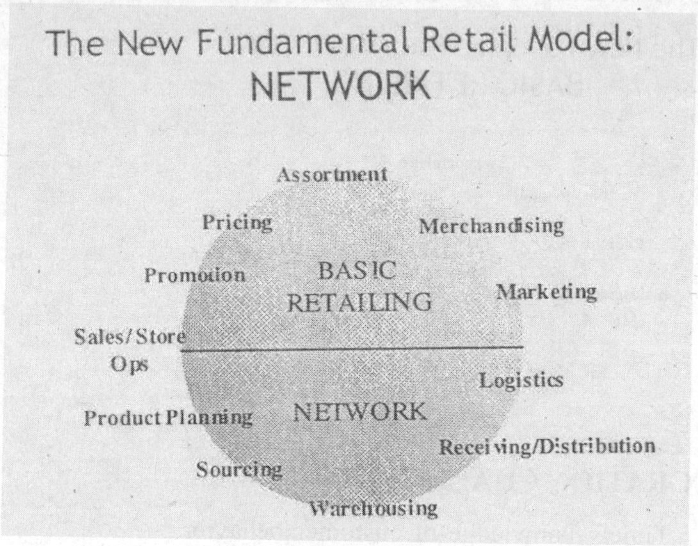

INTEGRATION CHALLENGES

- Lack of awareness of basic retailing initiatives
- Lack of connection to customer activity
- Lack of forward visibility
- Timely access to KPIs
- Advance alerts to changes and decisions taken on the fly
- Exchange of information with vendors

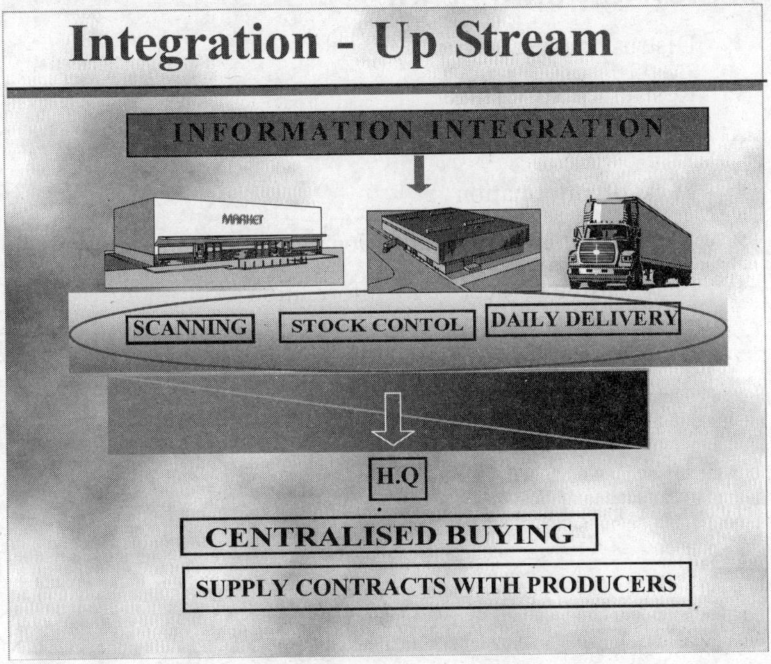

The New Fundamental Retail Model
"The Full Cycle"

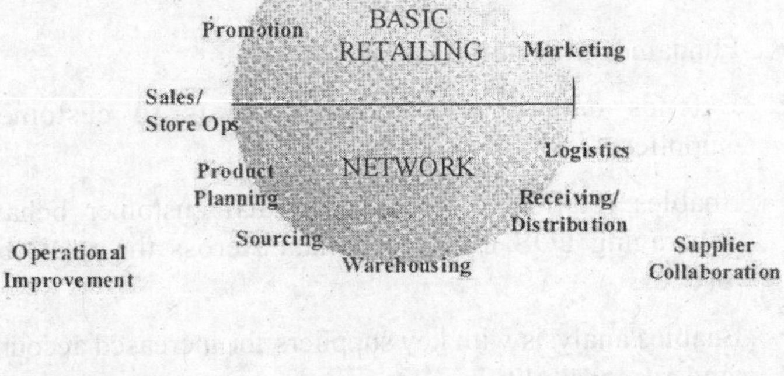

INTEGRATION CHALLENGES

- Distrust among parties
- Resistance to change
- Loss of customer focus
- Lack of information
- Timely exchange of information between retailer and suppliers
- Easy customer access to information
- Access to appropriate KPIs and analytics

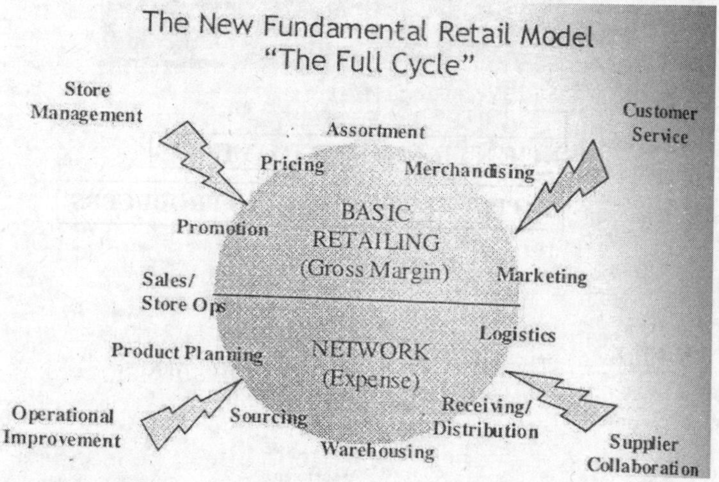

CONCLUSION

- Fundamental Retailing Pays Off
- Extends data access and/or analysis to customers and suppliers
- Enables retailers to focus on actual customer behavior by leveraging POS transaction data Across the retail business process.
- Enables analysis with key suppliers for increased accountability and responsibility

and ultimately thrive in a challenging competitive environment.

MULTI-CHANNEL: THE NEW RETAIL MODEL

"A new, superior retailing model is emerging in a number of countries. It is not simply about executing the same activities in multiple, separate channels" This model provides multi-channel options to market, sell, deliver, provide service and communicate. The Store environment and promotional activities are also have several options. Web, Catalogue, SMS.Digital media and Local Area Marketing and the nature of Competitions all aspects are given attention from customers' considerations. "Mere presence does not constitute a effective retail store". It is observed that 30% of consumer purchasing decisions are pre-planned; the remaining are made on the spot .Increased numbers of people are suffering 'product claustrophobia' because they simply cannot choose which brand to buy from the dozens on offer. Therefore, something is needed to persuade them to purchase.

The effectiveness of a store channel depends upon a number of factors.These may be as follows:

- Environment
- Service
- Stock level performance
- Category management
- Market responsiveness
- CRM

How effective this model will be- depends upon not the presence of multi channels but on the nature and its suitability in optimization of

How effective this model will be- depends upon not the presence of multi channels but on the nature and its suitability in optimization of the profit."

NETWORK MARKETING

Multi-level marketing (MLM) or network marketing is a business model where the selling of products depends on the people in the network. Not only is a product being sold, but other salespeople are being recruited to sell that same product or product line.It''s probably not a type of business one would initially consider when discussing retail businesses, but Amway used this model quite successfully for many years.

Commercial retail locations are available in many different forms. Stop and think about the businesses in your town.Like most communities, there are probably older shopping areas, new bustling retail locations and some tucked away shops.

Retailers have many store location factors to consider when choosing a place for their business. Here are a few of the more common types of retail locations.

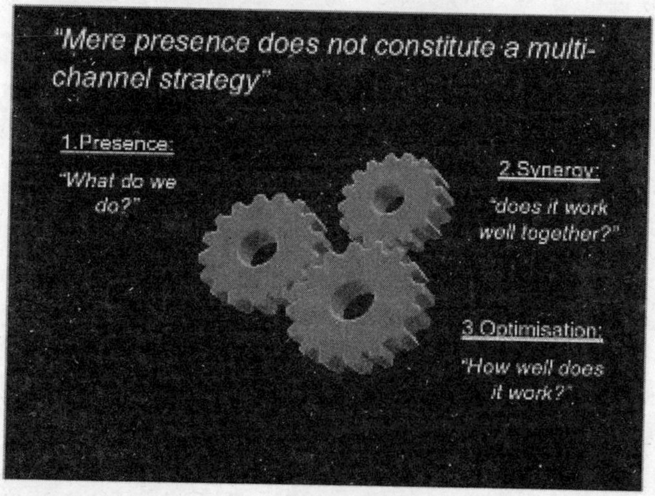

PROMOTION :

It is now realized that the success of store lies in*"making promotions more effective"Although all retailers undertake promotional activities ,however,* many retailers don't measure 'promotion profitability', They simply aim at only volume lift via promotion whereas the effectiveness does not lie on increasing volume. It is noted that as few as 10%-20% or promotions are profitable

Even with successful promotions, promoted item are out .of stock as much as 10% of the time.This will affect their profitability.The focus should be on promotion profitability. However, b*oth retailers and consumer goods companies are failing to optimise their promotional activity. Many times the increased promotional activities lead to* 'Promotion fatigue' – which refers to a situation where *the constant promotional activities by retailers and manufacturers have resulted in consumers growing weary at the sight of more promotions.The new model tries to avoid this situation.. This model suggests for* defining best offer for each customer rather than mailing every available offer"

An appropriate and innovative promotional "Campaigns can generate up to 1/3 more profit at the same cost of previous campaigns." The most important factors are following -

- **Which *channel?***
- **Which *message?***
- **What *frequency?***
- **What's *unique about it?***
- **Who *receives it?***
- **Why*?***

Will I use it the same, more, less, differently?

CATALOGUE

Although catalogue marketing is regarded as one of the method of effective retailing.These retailers usually specialize in hard goods such as houseware, jewellery, etc.In such a system, the customer walks into the retail showroom and goes through the catalogue from which he chooses the product.The use of catalogues as a retailing in the Indian context can help many established brick and mortar retailers to extend their area of operation to small towns. It is observed that **Some retailers spend as much of 60% of their marketing budgets on Catalogue Marketing in big cities.**

This type of retailing is required to consider a number of factors to become successful.

- Frequency of new catalogues
- The number of competitors and their strategy.
- Quality of products and services
- The degree of differentiation
- The capability of targeting
- The message sent to the customers
- Steady growth in unaddressed catalogues
- Ability to closely target a catchments area or demographic/ lifestyle dimensions predominantly used as a 'call to store'
- This model is being adopted by several retailers with great success.

LOCAL AREA MARKETING

Local Area Marketing is any activity conducted at the individual outlet level.It recognises that every area is unique.It Starts with an understanding of the local market. This model Identifies and exploits unique local opportunities. It uses the right tools to reach the right people at the right place at the right time. It focuses on improved targeting and local relevance.It actually leverages local strengths, knowledge and relationships It.

§ Starts with an understanding of the local market

§ Identifies and exploits unique local opportunities

§ Uses the right tools to reach the right people at the in the right place at the right time

§ Focuses on improved targeting and local relevance

§ Leverages local strengths, knowledge and relationship.

For example, at McDonald's, the 'Quick-EST' model is crucial, because being close and convenient to where the customers live, work, and shop helps us create maximum value.If you want to harness your company's strengths to become a leader in your category–and stay in tune with what your customers want. Ander and Stern in their book "Winning at Retail" warn of the 'treacherous middle' into which retailers too easily drift.They provide a thoughtful approach to retail differentiation.

(See Winning At Retail: Developing a Sustained Model for Retail Success— Willard N. Ander (Author), Neil Z. Stern)

Today's top retailers all have one thing in common – they establish defined market positions for themselves, and carve out a particular place in the customer's mind.In short, they dedicate themselves to being the best at something and they defend that advantage at all costs.The savviest retailers know that trying to be everything to everyone can not work for every retailer.

The Est model guides business leaders in making their company the best in one of five critical areas

§ assortment (biggest),

§ price (cheapest),

§ fashion (hottest),

§ customer service (easiest),

§ and speed of service (quickest).

Establishing a position as a leader in one of these five areas is ultimately the secret of success for Wal-Mart, Kohl's,Target, and other winning retailers.

This model suggests the strategy to become effective in an area particularly where customers are not homogenous– as they normally are.

WAL-MART'S INTERNATIONAL RETAIL MODEL

WalMart the world's largest retail company is operating in a number of countries including India. The success of WalMart is attributed to its international model. The foremost factor which has been the company, concentrating is the customer. *Don Sonderquist, former CEO Wal-Mart* Stores observed that "Regardless of where we are, customers want to be treated well, want to have a good assortment of products to choose from and they want merchandise at a great price. The most amazing fact is that our associates around the world embrace and protect this culture that they have built over the last thirty five years"

A number of factors are attributed to the success of WalMart, however the major ones are-

- Efficient operations with gradual expansion and extension.
- Low cost strategy
- Lower Cost Of Goods through aggressive volume buying and
- Global procurement
- Efficient logistics
- Higher inventory turnover through volume selling
- Store focused/store-within-a-store operations
- Continuous merchandising
- Global branding
- Consumer
- Responding to important store choice attributes of locational convenience, price, assortment, service and community.
- Corporate culture
- Inspirational leadership and corporate culture

- Capacity for innovation and reinvention
- Extensive internal communications
- Base in large U.S. market

These strategies together with considerations for local culture and competitors forms a model.

WalMart model is considered as the best model for adoption throughout the world and particularly by developing countries. The model has following important characteristics.

An extremely efficient production process.

Streamlined operations–from buying products, distributing them to stores. Selling .

"Just in time "strategy at all levels thereby reducing cost The process forms a continuous chain.The modern technology is used to monitor and manage inventory.

A well developed effective information system.

The pricing technique is regarded as the most practical when the product is offered at a competitive price. Achieving cost leadership by low wage strategies, unskilled jobs, imposition of two tiered wage systems and substitution of contingent for full time workers.Collaborating with big companies of other countries and focusing on revenue, not on label. 75% of WalMart's revenule came from stores that don't come under the WalMart label.This model is a structuring model based on technology and process instead of developing human resources.

COMPETENCY MODEL

This model is based upon the general concept of competency. For performing any activity the desired competencies are necessary therefore for retail sector certain competencies are to be identified which are pre-requisites of success of retailing.This model suggests 4 types of competencies as given below.

COMPETENCIES BY THE RETAIL INDUSTRY

TOP-LEVEL SUMMARY OF COMPETENCY MODEL FRAMEWORK

Tier 1: Personal Effectiveness

Interpersonal Skills

Integrity

Adaptability/Flexibility

Motivation

Dependability and Reliability

Willingness to Learn

Tier 2: Academic Competencies

Reading for Information

Business Writing

Mathematics

Basic Computer Skills

Communication: Listening and Speaking

Locating and Using Information

Tier 3: Workplace Competencies

Business Fundamentals

Teamwork

Professionalism

Marketing /Customer Focus

Planning and Organizing

Problem Solving/Decision Making

Applied Technology

Tier 4: Industry-wise Technical Competencies

Sales

Customer Service

Merchandising/Retailing

Operations

Human Resources

With these competencies retailer can get success.This is obvious that if one possess a number of competencies in the area, the success is bound to come until and unless some external unmanageable crisis does not emerge.The advantage of this model lies in enumerating nature of competencies required in the field of retailing.

STRATEGIC PROFIT MODEL

This model is aimed at focusing on profit to the retailer which is the ultimate goal of any business.The model rests on the premise that the performance of the retailer is obtained by looking into the financial criteria such as return on investment, sales or profits and retailer's unique capabilities.

Since the capital investment in retailing has to be high to become competitive the financial management becomes critical factor.First of all, retailer has to determine the performance objective which will atleast include following:

The desired performance which should be translated into a numerical goal that should be achieved.

The time period within which the same is to be achieved.

The resources both competencies and material, required to achieve the objectives.

The appropriate strategy and activities to be performed to achieve the objectives.

The retailer should assess the total assets and calculate the net profit. The performance can be judged by the following ratio –

Return on Assets = Net Profit / Total assets.

This return on assets can be viewed in terms of –

Profit path which is measured by the net profit margin.This indicates the amount of profit after tax (pat) that a firm earns, divided by its net sales.

Turnover path which is measured by asset turnover.This measures the productivity of a firm's investment in assets and is expressed in terms of net profit divided by total assets.

A retailer may earn high profit either by turnover path or by profit path.

Profit Path

Ultimately, the objective is to maximize net profit since that is the measure of firm's overall performance.To understand and calculate the **net profit** few concepts are to be understood clearly.

Net Sales – It is the total amount of Rupees received by a retailer after making payment of all refunds to customers for returned merchandise and customer allowances.This can be expressed as –

Net sales – Gross amount of sales-Customer returns-Customer allowances.

Customer returns – Refers to the value of merchandise that customers return due to any reasons such as being damaged, do not fit, etc.

Customer allowances – Refers any additional price reduction given to the customer

Gross Margin – It is also called Gross profit made on merchandise sales and can be found by-

Gross margin = Net sales- cost of goods sold.

This does not consider the expenses associated with operating the store.

Gross margin may be expressed as a percentage of net sales to which will help in comparing the performance of various types of merchandisethe performance of one organisation with other retailers.

Gross margin / Net sales = Gross margin% .

(3) **Expenses** – This refers to costs incurred in running the business.These include – Selling expenses, general expenses, interest paid, and administrative expenses.

(4) **Net Profit** – Net profit is a measure of the firm's overall performance.

Net Profit = Gross margin - Expenses.

This can be expressed either before or after tax.Ultimately the net profit is calculated after taxes since that is the amount which will be available to retailer either for reinvestment and/or for disbursing as dividends to shareholders .

Turn over Path

To proceed to this path, the retailer has to analyze the balance sheet.The balance sheet summarizes a retailer's financial position at a given point of time.

It shows the following relationship:

Assets = Liabilities + Owner's equity.

With the help of the analysis of data one can find out the asset turnover which is–

Asset turnover = Net Sales/Total assets.

Here, it should be understood that fixed assert do not turn over as quickly as inventory. Asset turnover can be used to evaluate and compare how effectively manger uses his assets.

The strategic profit model helps retailers since it combines two major decision making areas–profit margin in management and asset management.This helps in understanding the inter relationship between these two.The limitation is that this model uses return on asses as the primary criterion for planning the firm's financial performance. Nevertheless, this model is useful in evaluating financial implications of new strategic decisions before they are implemented.

TOTAL TOUCH MODEL

The new demanding consumer has higher needs and expectations from life.The result is the "I want it better, cheaper, easier, faster, and now" consumer who knows that if he/she can't have these demands met by your business there are a dozen alternatives.Therefore there is a need for retailers to have a model that meets the demands of the "I want it better, etc." shopper – one that they can reach out and touch and be touched at any time and place.To stick to a one-channel distribution strategy makes about as much sense as running a marketing campaign with only one medium.

Retailing Total Touch Model

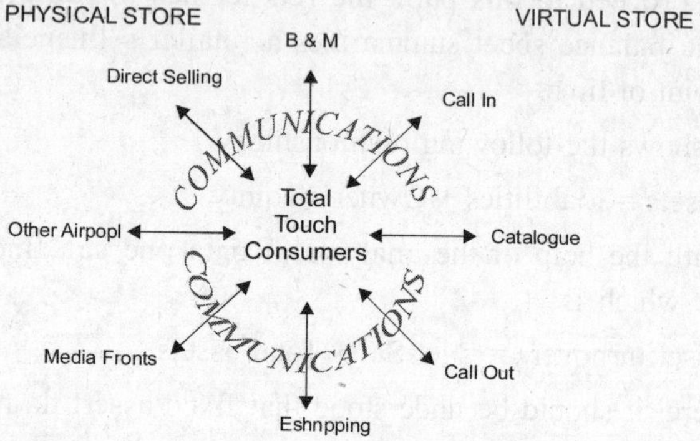

Source : J. C. Williams.

This Total Touch Model is simple and obvious. So what retailers, manufacturers, shopping centres, etc. must do is come to grips with the reality of the changing channels and their sales usage, shifts, and opportunities. The need to embrace and deal with a multi-channel, Total Touch strategy seems obvious:

People shop across channels. We are not channel bound today:

So offer multi-channel choice.

Be prepared to manage customer relationships as they shop and communicate with you across several channels.

E-retailing is setting new high standards for pricing, product, assortments, information, ease of shopping, services, and speed:

Ensure that you have similar policies, practices, and standards across all of your channels – or risk alienating customers.

Not embracing or testing a new channel for fear of cannibalization is foolish:

Play a market share game because your competitors are.If you don't, they will take market share from your basic/traditional channel and block you from new channels.

Very importantly, in a proliferation of channels, stores, and Web sites, a powerful brand will be one of the most important keys to success:

B & M retailers have a huge advantage if they capitalize on their established brand power.

This has been termed as Retail EST Model.It simply states that to win, a retailer has to be the best (the strategic differentiator) in one of several retail offerings.This is described as clearly positioning the company in one or more of the preferred locations to win.The losers are not best at anything, gravitate to central "all things to all people" position, and are sucked into the Black Hole of retailing – never to return again.

It should be clear that in the world of intense competition the differentiation vanishes during a short time since all competitors are

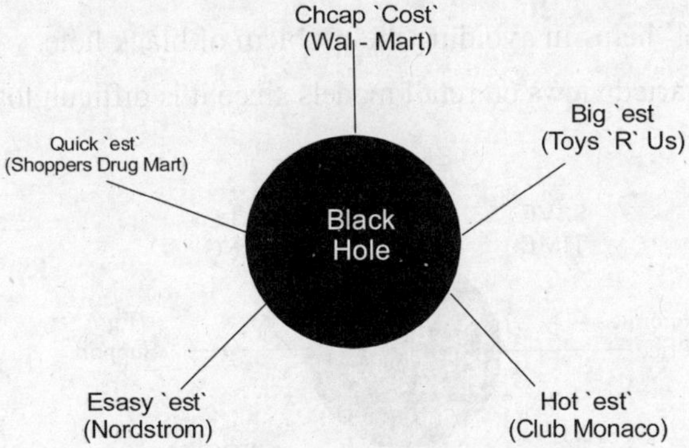

interested in targeting the customers.That is why, many retailers are lost in the said black hole.

A NEW STRATEGIC MODEL

The simplicity of the Retail EST model makes it compelling.It seems more logical that the entire approach should focus on consumer and his needs and expectations.The simple question arises what most shoppers want now more than ever ? Obviously in their hyper-busy lives, they are looking for solutions to time, money, well-being, self-esteem, and social experiences.When Retailers expect that shoppers should revisit for better assortments, or service, or Experience becomes meaningless since it is a one-dimensional approach that is retail-centric rather than shopper-centric Retailer should try to address the problems of shoppers that his store is going to do for them.That the store can offer a solution to their wants/needs. Retail businesses should be built on a multi-dimensioned format that delivers solutions to the shoppers to —

save me time = efficiency,

save me money = low price,

enhance my well-being and self esteem = ego support, and

give me special social contacts = an experience.

This solutions approach to retail strategies forces retailers to think not only in terms of the many factors that provide a solution, but also the retail channels that can do it best. And of course the company's core strategy needs to be deliverable in each channel!

This model helps in avoiding the problem of black hole.

There are varied views on retail models since it is difficult to identify

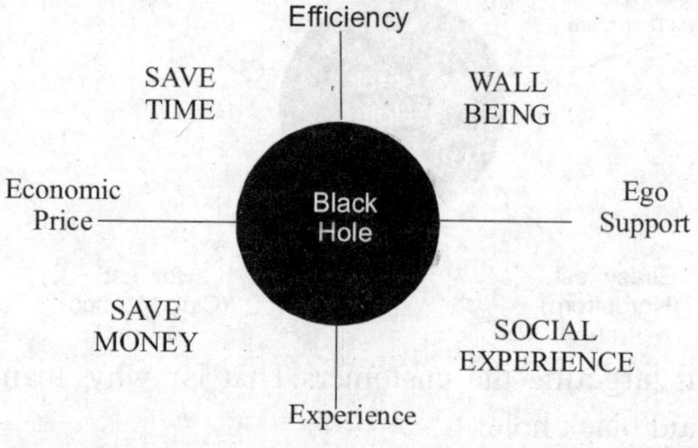

the most suitable and appropriate model which is applicable in different locations and at different times. Richard Fenker, Vice President and Chief Software Architect of Market Insite Group.Dr.Fenker, formerly the founder of Tangram Corporation of U.S. opined that no one seems to understand all the issues that relate to modeling.He observed that "the biggest of these issues, is that any modeling that I've every seen, only scratches the surface of how people are actually behaving." Some others feel that **the models do not factor the human behavior on the competitive side. Many of the models in use employ sales figures from the store in which the model was being formulated and did not factor the relationship to competitive environment.**

If we examine, various gravity models over the last 15 years, we could see that it worked in some cases but in most cases, it had limited utility. The approach we adopted in the early '90s was to begin to pull from the shelf of all possible models, and to use each model selectively to describe certain kinds of behaviour. If we divide the world into those that buy our products and those that buy competitor's products.

If we look at the behaviour people who live in a rural town, where demand is controlled by who lives around the store, then a model may work well..But as we move to city stores, suburban stores, mall stores, lots of fluid behavior is observable within the market.The models work well when things do not undergo change but in practical life everything changes. As soon as one moves any modeling into real world situations in markets where there one gets city stores, suburban stores, mall stores, lots of fluid behavior within the market is noticed and the model becomes meaningless.

The Future of Retailing

Everyone feels that the future of retailing is bright and even in developing country like India its share will increase fast in a short period. Today's consumers are more informed, more discerning, with more choices…and more power. They are more attentive to the benefits and consequences of food. Today's consumer's have challenged us like no other generation of consumers and have made us better at what we do in order to serve their needs.

A nutritional correction is taking place today – beauty definedon how you feel, not on how you look

The following forces have become critical for retailers and their brands

Market Forces

Shopper Lifestyles & Behaviours – This is one of the most critical area. The retailers need to assess the present and future life styles and behaviour of shoppers. The theories and studies on consumer behaviour may help a retailer.

Technology: The technology is improving and changing rapidly.The retail industry has to adopt the new technology at the earliest.The competition will take place in this area.

Globalization: As already discussed, globalization is influencing the life style and consumer behaviour to a great extent. It has also affected the supply side and the nature of marketing.

Speed: The customer has time to wait.The speed is the urgent need in every area whether it is the question of supply chain, adoption of technology, convenience and entertainment provisions of stores,or the customer service and custömer care.

Capital markets: The organized retailing is capital intensive therefore capital market is important.

Competitive Forces

Consolidation, Concentration, Substitution –The retailer has to decide the course of action in light of the competition .

Saturation – Considering the size of market and number of competitors one has to take into account the problem of saturation before entering or expanding the business.

Impact of Discounters: Discounting is one of the effective practice resorted by retailers to attract customers however there need to assess the issue of margin compression that will tell upon the profitability of the orgnisation.

Labor relations and productivity –As the size of store/ organization increases the problems relating to labour relations and productivity becomes critical.

Demand Driven Supply Chains-The supply chain is a known critical factor in retailing. Any breakdown or delay in supply is disastrous for a retail store.

The future and success will depend upon.

- Right Assortment
- Fresh
- Ancillary

- Apparel
- All other Food
- Right merchandising
- Department & Category
- Strategies for
- Private label
- Pricing and promotion
- Localization
- New products/store
- Right marketing
- Clear consumer target
- Clear positioning
- Marketing Overlays
- In and out of store media platforms
- Vendor tie-ins/co-marketing

Challenges

Retail business facing forces of unprecedented change in an increasingly complex selling environment–These may be summarized as under-

(a) Challenging economy

Inter-channel and intra-channel competition has increased considerably. Explosive growth in super centers and malls has provided opportunity to customers. Growing neighborhood market concept is developing fast.

Business is getting tougher due to increased competition from big giants like Wal-Mart, the world's largest retailer Shoppers are shopping across channels and at multiple retailers within channels.

(b) Changing consumer lifestyles –

Increased income, dual earning nuclear families, empowerment and freedom to women, more women in jobs, small size of family, influence of television and western fashion have changed the lifestyle of the consumers in a big way.

Today's consumers are demanding three things

(a) Weight Management Information and products

(b) Health and Nutrition Information and products

(c) Wellness Solutions

(d) Entertainment with convenience.

(d) Labour supply and cost issues –

Labour cost becomes 8-12% depending on format.The problem of skilled and efficient labour supply too is a big challenge before retail industry.Stringent rules are responsible for increasing the cost.It is estimated that health Insurance costs is increasing –14% per year.

(c) Governmental regulation –

Increased Government regulations at state and national levels Is noted throughout the world. With the growth of retail and other macro variables, the government is resorting to more and more taxation, tort reform, changes in trucking/driver laws, etc.

(d) Technology –

e-tailing, i-giving, kiosks, mining data warehouse information Technology, etc. are putting serious challenges before the industry and future depends upon these. Expensive technology needed to compete and target market/differentiate from competitors.

(e) Capital requirements

Since the entire scenario has changed and store design to customers' expectations changed radically therefore the capital requirement during next 5 years to exceed those of the past 20 years.

(f) Retailer consolidation –

Industry experts predict that sooner independents will not exist 5 years from now. Why?

Because the trend reveals that–

(a) Retailer consolidation continues

(b) Regional chains continue to dominate

(c) Lack of succession plan.

(g) Competition :

"You can beat Wal-Mart, but you must do it with the right approach. If you're battling Mike Tyson, you want to challenge him to a game of chess – not a boxing match." Observes – Professor John Stanton of St. Joseph's University, US. However, it is not possible in case of retailing since all competitors are operating in the same field. Competition is a big challenge however it provides opportunity too.

- Competition makes an organization better.
- It makes retailers sharper, alert, more innovative and creative.
- It often creates newfound energy in an organization.
- Competition gives customers a better shopping experience.

*However,as–Tom Jackson,Ohio Grocers Assn observes– "Competition is a little like alcohol – in moderation it's relaxing and good for your heart.In excess,alcohol is destructive."*Too much competition can be detrimental to growth and progress:

It can create a defeated attitude or a "why bother trying"mentality.

While it prunes poor operators from the marketplace, it can destroy good operators, as well, thus reducing choice for consumers.

How Competition Hurts and Helps To Inspire Change

A look at various supermarket retailers operating in various countries one can identify the following.

Architects: The big guns, whether by dint size or influence, that have set the standards for retailing and whose moves will have ripple effects across the field.

Achievers: Food retailers that wield power in their corners of the industry, that broke new ground in jpast and that are likely to make news in coming years.

Strivers: Those companies facing acute challenges, among them toiling to recover lost ground, emerge from mediocrity, or just hang on to fight another day. The next few years hold the potential of making of breaking some of these operators.

The supermarket industry is repositioning itself for growth.Those operators who are focusing on fresh, reducing inventory levels, and investing in customer service and technology are not just surviving – they're thriving.

"If you're doing business the same old way, it's probably not the right way."

How to succeed in fast-changing, challenging times?

- Driving revenue—accelerating brand growth—is the imperative for retailers and manufacturers
- Retailers need more and better business intelligence to do this
- Increase successful new product introductions, speed-to-shelf

- Provide support for localized community marketing events
- Retailers open and eager for help in pulling consumers, making supermarkets destination of choice, stimulating purchase and driving higher satisfaction.

Focus on three sectors:

Experts feel that in India following 3 sectors need focus –

(1) Food/restaurants;

(2) Convenience items (i.e.,variety, healthy beauty aids, basics apparel);

(3) Specialty or lifestyle shops (i.e., gourmet wine, cheese, frige, A.C, etc.)

Potential For Growth

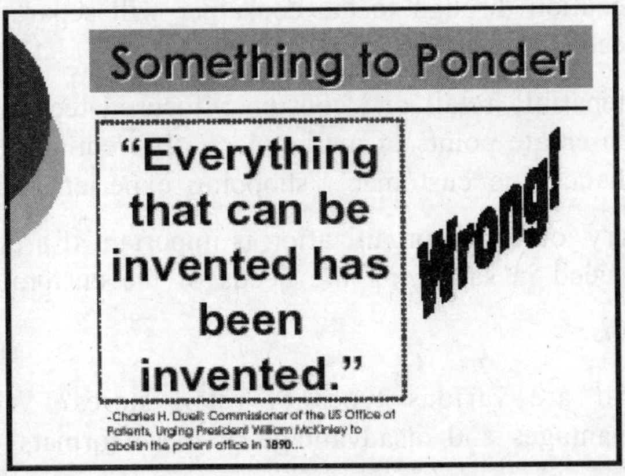

With so much diversity in formats and execution at retail, the balance of the supply chain is a key component in differentiation and success.

- Simply having the right format will not ensure success.
- Execution through to the consumer will separate those who succeed from those that do not.
- Compatible retail and consumer focused technologies can also create points of marketplace differentiation as they can enhance the customer's shopping experience.
- Every job in the organization is important if a company is to succeed in satisfying the needs of the customer

Questions:

1. What are various types of retail stores? What are the advantages and disadvantage of these formats?
2. What difficulties might an independent encounter if it tries to expand into a chain?
3. Why would a department store want to lease space to an outside operator rather than run a business. What are the risk in it.?
4. What are the basis of classification of retail stores?
5. Compare between a small independent store and a mall.

6. How Competition hurts and helps To inspire change in retailing?
7. Discuss various models of retailing. Which one you should suggest for India.
8. "There are a number of theories of retailing however it is difficult to endorse any one as the most appropriate. Discuss."
9. What is the future of retailing in general.?
10. What future you see of retailing in India?

CHAPTER 4

Retail– Organisation Design and Structure in Retail

Every organization whether big or small needs a organizational design and structure.The organization structure is a formal system through which a retail firm assigns tasks/ functions, policies, resources, authority, responsibilities and rewards to achieve its goals and satisfy the needs of its target market.In fact, a firm cannot survive unless its organisation structure satisfies the target market. As the size and variety increases the problem becomes complex.The structure of an organization is a formal system which identifies and determines the roles and functions of each section and employee in achieving the goal of the organization. It defines the authority as well as responsibility of each employee and the activities to be performed by him.In general in retail sector these activities can be classified as –

- Top Management.
- Strategic management.
- Merchandise management
- Store management
- Operations management, i.e., Administration and Human resources.
- Finance and Accounts.
- Support functions, e.g., Advertising, Marketing PR and accounts.

Thus, organization is a formal structure of roles and positions put in place to achieve some specific goals.The structure of a retail organization defines the role of employees and the way in which the organization functions.This chapter discussed the steps involved in designing an appropriate retail organization structure to enhance a store's ability to serve its target markets. To design an effective retail organization structure, managers/ owners must define store objectives, identify the tasks, classify the tasks and jobs, and assign responsibilities and authority to various positions, and define the relation between them.

Organizations can have flat structures or vertical (tall) structures. A flat organization structure has only one or two levels of management, whereas a vertical organization has more than two levels of management. The performance of retail sector is influenced by its organisation structure.

It is obvious that the performance of retail sector depends largely upon the effectiveness of this structure. Let us examines the various types of organization structures that which exist in retail sector.

While developing the organization design a number of aspects have to be considered.

- ✦ Defining the organizational goal.
- ✦ Tasks to be performed.
- ✦ Determining the need for specialists in various areas.
- ✦ Selection and recruitment of right person.
- ✦ Designating various position and reporting relationship.
- ✦ Financial implications of the structure.

The increasing competition,increasing expectations of the customers, need to respond faster to consumer needs and wants and pressures on costs and margins influence the decision regarding organization structure.The role of technology also taken into account.

Guidelines for Organization Structure

1. **Fulfilling needs of Target Market**
   - There should be sufficient personnel to provide appropriate customer service.
   - Personnel should be knowledgeable and courteous.
   - Store facilities are well maintained.
   - The specific needs of branch store customers met.
   - Changing needs are promptly addressed.
2. **Needs of Employee**
   - Positions are challenging and satisfying adequately.
   - Orderly promotion program.
   - Employee participation in the decision making.
   - Clear and open communication channels.
   - Clear authority responsibility relationship.
   - The line of authority should be traceable, i.e., chain of command be clear.
   - Fair treatment with employees.
   - Scheme of reward and punishment.
3. **Needs of Management and Organisation.**
   - Process of selection and ability to retain competent personnel.
   - Adequately defined personnel procedures and policies.
   - Each worker need to report to only one supervisor.
   - Operating departments have adequate staff support.
   - Levels of organisation are properly developed.
   - Goal of organization are well defined and integrated.
   - Absenteeism is low.
   - A system to replace personnel in an orderly manner.

- Flexibility to adapt to changes in customers or the environment.

Types of Organization Structure

As pointed out, various factors influence the creation of organizational structure which may be:

- Scope and scale of operation, viz., local, regional, national or international.
- Types and nature of products sold
- Type of departmentalization, i.e., product wise or location wise.
- Thus, organization structures vary from one retailer to another.

Organization structure of small Stores/ Independent Retailers/ Single stores, etc.

Inspite of increasing importance of organized retailing from departmental stores to big malls, still the small, independent stores exist in almost every country but largest number are found in our country. The kirana shop, the boutique, furniture, hardware, shoe store dairy shop, etc. are the examples of these stores.Normally in such a store, one person is the owner cum manager. He is responsible for most of the aspects of retail operation.The family members usually assist him. In a number of cases, a few sales persons are also engaged.If the size increases, the external advisors and back office staff are also engaged in such stores. It must be remembered that such independent stores need not necessarily be small in size.In that case the number of assistants increases.In such a situation, the organisation structure is defined specifically and the duties and responsibilities are identified.The back office is also engaged and the help of computer is also availed of Mostly the decision maker is the owner relating to goals, merchandising, pricing, advertisement, hiring of staff etc.

Owner/Manager
Responsibilities
Buying, Promotion, Sales, HR, Operational control, General Management.

Owner

Manager

External advisors
Lawyers, Chartered Accountant Bankers,etc

Back office staff
Responsibilities
Accounting & Record Keeping, Data Entry, Inventory control, Purchase Orders, Time Keeping & Payroll, Facilities Management.

Sales staff
Responsibilities
Customer Service, Selling Stock Control, Display and Housekeeping.

(Structure of a Retail Store Chain/Department Store/etc.)

Increase in the size and operation units by big stores is a common phenomenon.When the number of stores that a retailer operates increases, the management becomes complex which affects the structure too.The Retail store chains may operate in a city, regional, national or an international level. Such stores may be departmentalized on the basis of functions or product lines.The number and type of personnel would depend on the size, nature and area of operation.The structure is also changed accordingly since structure is determined by the tasks performed by the retailing firm.

As back as 1927, a functional organisation structure for such stores has been suggested by Paul Mazur– known as "Mazur Plan." (See Paul M. Mazur, Principles of organisation Applied to Modern Retailing.) He identified four major functions of a retail store and proposed the structure around them.He considered that these four functions are found in every retail organisation irrespective of the size. He identified these four functions-

Merchandising: This is one of the most important department and its duties start with forecasting the merchandise required, procuring the same, pricing it and ensuring availability in the store, etc.

Publicity: It includes various activities of marketing such as advertisement, sales promotions, public relations, publicity, etc.

Operations: As the name suggests, activities like actual operations of the store, receiving the goods, checking, maintaining records and maintaining customer relations, etc

Control: It comprises several activities such as accounting, credit, regulation etc.The department of control is responsible for looking after the assets and liabilities of the organsiation.subsequently a number of other functions such as supply chain management, logistics and Human Resource Management have been added to the above 4 functions.

A retail firm would want to structure and assign task, policies and resources in order to meet the ever-changing needs of the firms target market, employees and management. Now, retail organizations have prioritized retention and growth of employees within the organization due to high attrition and demand for skilled work force.There are a few steps that form the core of HR Practice in retail.

Outline the specific tasks among channel members and customers. Grouping the tasks into jobs.Classifying the jobs.Finally integrating the position in the organizational charts.

The specific tasks mentioned above deals with a number of activities which a retail firm undertakes such as setting prices shipping merchandise, logistics, research, marketing, customer interaction, sales, follow up services. According to the needs, these tasks may be outsourced or divided among the retailer, manufacturer middle men and so on.

After the retailer determines the tasks which it would perform, they are grouped into jobs such as sales persons, cashier, merchandisers, display personnel, store managers and marketing executives.Each organization has a different structure and culture hence the certain jobs could be clubbed as on. For example, the merchandise department would deal with display as well as procurement.

The organsiation structure is also formed on the basis of: Product lines which are offered, like appliances, jewellery, furniture, etc. Regional operations, i.e., the geographic departmentalization.In such structure, the personnel are responsible for activities in a certain region, state or nation.

A combination of these may also be built by retailers as per their needs.Thus diversified structure is also seen in the market.In such cases, the retailer operates more than on retail chain in more than one market. Pantaloon group is a good example of diversified retailing.

It should be remembered that the organisation structure must ensure proper utilization of manpower and healthy competition.

Considerations in developing Organisation Design: A number of factors need to be considered while developing the organisation design

(a) Employee's expertise and specialization

(b) Authority and responsibility

(c) Reporting relationships

(d) Retail strategy

(e) Degree of Centralisation

(f) Co-ordination of stores and merchandise.

(a)Employee's expertise and specialization

Individual expertise and specialization are considered while assigning the activities to him. An employee having expertise in managing supply chain should be assigned that task only. Because of the specialization in any area, employee will be performing better by using his unique skills and training. This will enhance the productivity

(b)Authority and responsibility:

It is necessary that responsibility and authority match to ensure efficiency. In case there is mismatch the performance will be affected adversely.This many times becomes a difficult task because of conflicting considerations. For example,specialization and matching authority with responsibility may not go together.

(c) Reporting Relationship

The reporting pattern and relationship are another important factor for consideration.The superior must have the appropriate number of employees, i.e., subordinates to report.Any deviation from the appropriate number will reduce the effectiveness of the organsiation.If number of subordinates increases, the superior will not be able to manage them properly and under utilization of capacity is apprehended.

(d) Retail strategy

Above all it is necessary that organisation structure must suit to the retail strategy. In an individual independent retail, the structure will be different as compared to a retail store chain.In a high competitive market the strategy will be different and the employees will be assigned different functions as compared to a non competitive location.

Degree of Centralisation

The decision making authority is significant in every organisation. The issue is to what extent the decision making is centralized or decentralized.By Centralisation, we mean that the decisions are taken by the corporate managers rather than by store, regional or area managers, whereas in decentralized system the authority is assigned to lower levels.

Co-ordination of stores and merchandise

The organizational structural should be such that matches and establishes co-ordination between merchandise and objectives of the unit. There should be co-ordination in all departments which is possible only when the organizational structure provides adequate provisions for this. The retail strategy should match with the structure.If the customers are price sensitive, the number of employees need to be limited whereas in case of other customers, the organisation structure should provide for more managers and decision making at the local store level.

Guiding Principles for organisation structure

Although it is difficult to identify an ideal or modal organisation structure, some basic guiding principles can be suggested which should look after the –

Market needs-

- The number of personnel should be adequate to provide appropriate customer service.
- The personnel should be knowledgeable and courteous.
- Store facilities must be well maintained.
- The specific needs of branch store customers are met.
- Provision for addressing changing needs of the market.

Management needs-

- There should be no mismatch between structure and strategy of the retail organisation.
- The levels of organisation are to be properly developed.
- It should relatively easy to obtain and retain competent personnel.
- The personnel policy and procedures be clearly defined.

Employee needs

- The positions must be challenging and satisfying enough.
- An orderly promotion program be provided.
- Employees should be able to participate in the decision making.
- The channels of communication should be clear and open.
- Faire treatment of each employee.
- Reward and punishment, i.e., stick and carrot policy should exist for motivation.
- The employees should be empowered to achieve the tareget.
- Retailers need
- The cost should be minimum.
- The image improving techniques could be adopted easily.

- The profitability is maintainable.
- Flexibility to restructure in times of slackness.

RETAIL FORMATS

As already discussed a retailer is that who buys goods or products in large quantities from manufacturers or importers,either directly or through a wholesaler, and then sells to end users or customers in small quantities.These are the shops and also called stores.Thus there is difference between wholesaling and retailing.

Wholesaling and Retailing

Wholesaling refers to all those activities which are involved in selling goods or services to those who buy for reselling or some business purpose. In fact wholesaling is in between manufacturing and retailing. Wholesaler buys from manufacturer in bulk and then sales to retailer. Wholesaler is a middleman or agent.The wholesalers include Merchants.

- Agent
- Brokers
- Jobbers
- Distributors

Functions of Wholesaler

In general, wholesaler performs following functions.

Buying and Assortment– He buys in bulk and build the assortments according to the needs of the market.

Bulk Breaking– He buys in bulk from the manufacturers and break the same into smaller units.

Selling and promoting– He helps manufacturer by keeping sales force and promoting goods at a relatively low cost.

Warehousing– He holds inventory thereby reduces the costs and risks of the manufacturer.

Transportation– He is able to transport products to a large number of retailers thereby ensures regular supply with the well established channel.

Economies of scale– By performing various functions, wholesaler provides to the customer various products at a cheaper cost because of economies of scale, transaction economies in terms of time and handling costs. The distribution cost is reduced because of large scale operations.

Retail Formats

The details relating to various types of retail formats and activities are already explained in Chapter III. However some of the issues relating to retail formats are discussed below-

Number of outlets: There can be Independent stores/shops as against chain stores.Independent retailers are those which have only one retail outlet.Such retailers have loyal large number of customers. They are able develop their own branding called store branding.

The others are chain stores: Normally retailers who operate in large number of outlets at various places are called chain stores.Thos which are having 11 or more units, are generally regional or national .They take full advantage of the economies of scale like wholesalers, e.g., centralized buying, standard stock list. Etc.

Multi Brand Outlet: Outlet which sells broad merchandise assortment are known as multi brand.The size may not be very large yet it is not too small.The objective is to have maximum display and fast inventory turnover and satisfy different types of customers having different brand preference.Such store target mainly to middle class customers who are interested in assortment breadth and moderate prices. Some of the features are–

- The merchandise quality may range from average to good.
- Price can be low/moderate/above average.
- Customer services may be minimum to above average.
- The assortment is not deep.

- The quality of merchandise, fixtures, fittings, visual communication and promotional tools may range from typical to innovative depending on location, competitors, etc.
- Normally the margin is low unless it enjoys the monopoly in the area.
- The entire layout, design and other fixtures etc. are determined on the basis of target market and merchandise.

Large Format Retailer

The large store keep popular brands of various qualities at a competitive price.The total area is large and it can accommodate an extensive assortment of goods.There are separate departments or floors along with innovative visual merchandise.It can be for a particular segment or for general category.

The sales force is large, trained and having coordination.

The store layout is carefully planned.

Shop-in-shop Retailer

Such an outlet has a huge layout and the objective is to bring a large number of retailers under one roof with the target of maximizing the footfalls.There are large blocks of independent retailers carrying major well known brands along with defined category mix. Innovative window displays, visual communication and measures of promotion are adopted.

Overall, it is able to attract a number of customers with alluring experience.Various other facilities such as dining, entertainment areas and ample parking space are some features of such outlet.

Exclusive Outlet

Such outlet is located strategically with a medium sized interactive layout. It sells a single focused category of products.The customers are brand conscious, individuals,cluster groups of same class with high loyalty.The customer service is given importance.

The comparative features of various outlet are presented in the Table given below.

Comparative features of different formats.

Features	Exclusive outlet	Multi Brand outlet	Large Format	Shop in shop
Breadth	Narrow	Broad	Moderately broad	Narrow
Depth	Deep	Narrow deep	Moderately	Shallow
Pricing Strategy	High	Low/ Moderate	Moderate/ High	Moderate/ High
Customer service	High	Low	Moderate/ High	Moderate/ High
Product Quality	High	Low/ High	Moderate/ High	Moderate/ High
Desirability	High	Low/ Moderate	Moderate	Low Moderate
Store Image	High	Low/ Moderate	High	Moderate/ High

Following factors also be considered while deciding about the retail format: -

1. Economic competition among retail operations is high as larger retail facilities attract and serve more customers coming from greater distances than small, local retailers.
2. With high levels of mobility and an awareness of shopping alternatives, customers may choose to shop outside of their local environments, though customers tended to concentrate shopping trips over weekly or biweekly periods of time for efficiency.
3. Though urban planners in many areas sought to create a self-sufficient town, residents frequently make purchases from retailers in greater metropolitan area.

4. The small number and limited variety of stores, as well as higher prices are the main reasons customers shopped outside of their locality.

5. A successful international retailer does not necessarily have to be a large retailer. Rather, a small and medium-sized (SME) retailer of specialist merchandise, endowed by a strong concept and format, is capable of overcoming any resource deficiencies associated by lack of size, with the ability to establish a fortuitous presence in international markets.

H.R. MANAGEMENT IN RETAIL

Retail is one of the labour intensive industry.Not only in the numbers, retail industry is employing verity of personnel in terms of nature, level and quality.Throughout the world retail is known for providing employment to a significantly high number of people having different level of competencies. It can be defined as The integration of all processes, programs, and systems in an organization that ensure staff are acquired and used in an effective way.

Importance of Human Resource Management

Since employee play a major role in performing critical business function, human resource management becomes too important. Since retailing is a service industry, retailers rely on people to perform the basic activities, e.g.,buying, displaying merchandise, providing service to customers to make them happy. Store personnel play a major role in attracting and retaining customers in a retail store.Without productive labor, no merchandise and operational plans can be successful.Store personnel are the most productive assets in a retail store, who can increase or decrease the store's profit.The quality and effectiveness of the organization is determined by the quality of the people that are employed.Success for most organizations depends on finding the employees with the skills to successfully perform the tasks required to attain the company's strategic goals.Management decisions and processes for dealing with employees are critical to ensure that the organization gets and keeps the right staff.

- Human resource management (HRM)can be the basis of a sustainable competitive advantage through human resource management.
- Labour costs account for a larger percentage of a retailer's expenses, which can be reduced by proper HRM.
- It is the behaviour and activities of employees which determine the nature of experience to the customer which ultimately responsible for sale and profit.
- The behaviour and support provided by the employees play a major role in differentiating a retailer's offering from its competitor.
- It is possible to copy out other factors but difficult to duplicate the behaviour of individuals.

Objectives of Human Resource Management

- Human resource management is key to the success of any retail organisation, it is undertaken with the following objectives:
- Human resource management attracts, develops, and maintains a talented workforce.
- Human resource management matches staffing with organizational needs.
- Top align the capabilities and behaviour of employees with the short terms and long terms goals of the retail firm.
- Performance management techniques appraise individual accomplishments and helps in measuring the performance through employee productivity.

These objectives are –

(a) Short term

– Increasing Employee Productivity

– Productivity = Sales/Number of Employees

(b) Long - term

– Increasing Employee Satisfaction

– Reducing Turnover

In case both the short and long objectives are not considered, that would lead to mismanagement of resources and may result in lower performance.Many corporate executives have said, "People are our most important asset" and that people determine the success and failure of the organisation.Inspite of this at times of declining profits and sales, they opt for decrease in labour costs.Generally, The number of employees is reduced, more part timers are hired, less qualified persons are recruited at a lower salary, lesser expenditure is incurred on training. Certainly in the short term the costs are reduced and margin may increase or lesser losses are registered. However, in the long run the profitability, image and credibility is affected adversely.The total performance hence sales are decreased because of these.

This becomes a spiral.Lower profitsà lesser employees—.Lower level employees —>.Demotivated employees—> à Lower sales —> lower profits.

One striking feature of personnel management in India is that the personnel are not given importance as this very sector is at the developing stage. Hence, retailers give less importance to In-Store Executives and also their training which is imparted by the experienced staff is inadequate.One must understand along with a good décor and environment, services are also important to make a mark in the customers mind. Hence, Quality of the services and how these services are provided to the customer becomes significant in our present times.

Scope of Human Resource Management

All major activities of an employee from the entry to the exit come under the purview of Human Resource Management.

- HRM planning
- Job analysis and design
- HRM planning

- Job analysis and design
- Job Description
- Job Specification
- Recruitment and selection
- Orientation/induction
- Socializing and Training new Store Employees
- Training and Development
- Performance Management
- Remuneration and benefits
- Compensation Program
- Motivation and Retention
- Welfare and safety
- Industrial Relations etc.

The organization is impacted by its environment. By paying careful attention to these facts, an organization can recruit competent, high-performing employees who are capable of sustaining their performance over the long term.You will also see that many factors, for example, globalization, technology, and demographics directly affect all management practices, but their effect is probably greatest in the management of human resources.This is because that whatever happens to an organization ultimately influences what happens to its employees.

The strategic Human Resource Management can be understood in context of organisation and the external environment by the diagram given below–

Strategic Human Resource Management

Human Resource Planning

Recruitment & Selection

Compensation & Benefits

Performance Appraisals

Training & Development

Human Resource Planning

"An effort to anticipate future business and environmental demands upon and organization and to provide personnel to fulfill that business and satisfy that demand" (Bowey, 1974).

Since it is important to have the right people in the right jobs at the right time, human resource planning is the process to achieve that. What the organization will do is make an assessment of the current capabilities of its employees, determine what it will need in the future, and design a program to meet those needs.

Depending on the organization's objectives and strategies, demand for human resources is contingent upon demand for the organization's products or services and on the levels of productivity. After estimating total revenue, management can estimate the number and kinds of human resources needed to obtain those revenues.

After it has assessed current capabilities and future needs, management can estimate future human resources shortages and over-staffing.Then, it can develop a program to match these estimates with forecasts of future labour supply.

Human Resource Planning

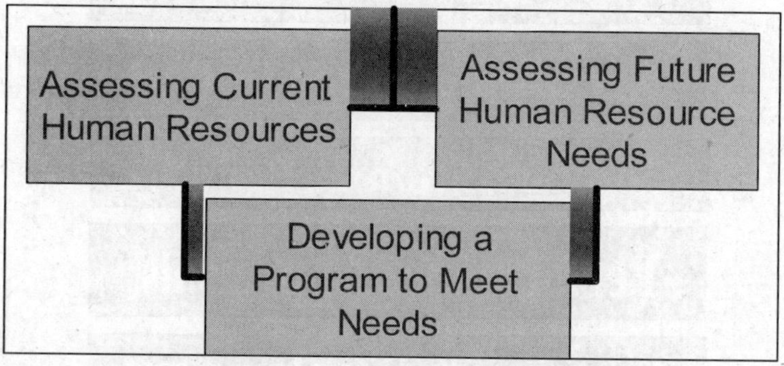

Recruitment

Once managers know their staffing needs,they can begin to look for capable people to fill those needs.The process to do this is called recruitment.It is a process that locates, identifies, and attracts capable candidates for the work. For many organizations, this has become a critical activity. As the business demands change, so do the skills required. And there are some skill sets that are in high demand which means organizations have to have a good plan to locate the people with the unique skills.Thus, Recruitment is Process of locating, identifying, and attracting capable candidates.

- Can be for current or future needs
- Critical activity for some corporations
- What sources do we use for recruitment.

But where do companies go to recruit employees? Many companies are finding new employees through the Internet.Organizations that are looking for people with a high-level of technological skills may focus their recruitment efforts by using the Internet.The web sites of organizations frequently have a link for enabling the browser to submit a resume.

The source that is used should reflect the labour market, the type or level of position, and the size of the organization. Are certain recruiting sources better than others? Recent studies have demonstrated that employee referrals generally produce the best candidates.This is because current employees screen applicants before referring them. Second, current employees believe that their reputations with the firm will be reflected in the candidates that they recommend; so, they refer only those who they believe will not make them look bad. Employee referrals, however, may not generate the diversity and mix of employees that is desirable.

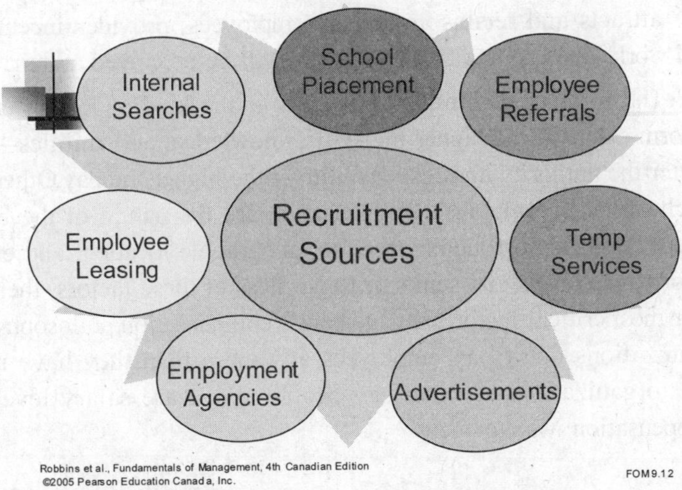

Selection

After the completion of the recruitment process, the manager needs to decide who to hire.Selection is essentially both a prediction exercise and a decision-making exercise.In the prediction exercise, the manager is predicting which applicant will be successful on the job is hired.The manager is also undertaking a decision-making exercise—choosing among choices.It is important to always keep in mind that the manager is selecting the person who can best meet the needs of the organization.

- Thus, it refers to
- Prediction exercise
- Thus, Not Perfect
- Decision-making exercise
- Purpose is to hire the person(s) best able to meet the needs of the organization
- Tied Back to Strategy
- Compensation Management

How does management decide who will get paid Rs.20 per day and who will receive RS.325,0000 per year?The answer lies in *compensation administration*: the process of determining a cost-effective pay structure that attracts and retains competent employees, provides incentives for hard work, and ensures that pay levels will be perceived as fair.

The primary determination of pay is the kind of job an employee performs: that is, the higher the skills, knowledge, and abilities—and the greater the authority and responsibility—the higher the pay.Other factors which influence employee compensation are the nature of the business, the environment surrounding the job, geographic location, and employee performance levels and seniority.Regardless of these factors, there is one other most critical factor: management's compensation philosophy. Some organizations don't pay employees any more than they have to while other organizations want to pay people above are salary levels.Thus, Compensation Management:

- Is a process of determining cost-effective pay structure
- Is designed to attract and retain
- Provide an incentive to work hard
- Structured to ensure that pay levels are perceived as fair–

Factors That Influence Compensation

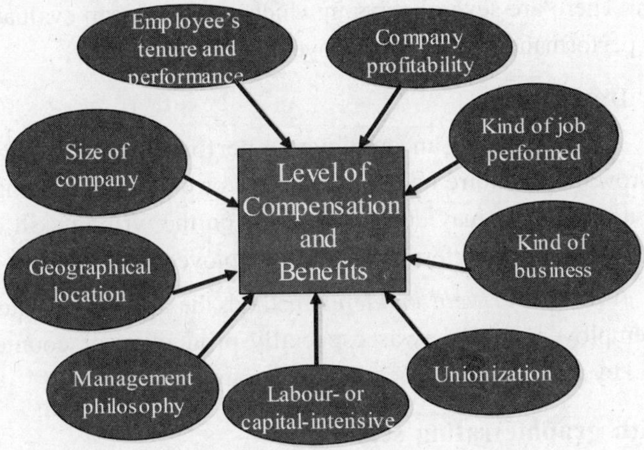

Robbins et al., Fundamentals of Management, 4th Canadian Edition
©2005 Pearson Education Canada, Inc.

There are a number of factors that can influenced compensation levels.The above figure displays the various factors.For example, private-sector jobs typically provide higher rates of pay than comparable positions in public and not-for-profit jobs.Likewise, employees who have been with an organization for a long time may have had a salary increase each year.

Since skill levels tend to affect work efficiency and effectiveness, many organizations implement skill-based or competency-based pay systems.These types of systems reward employees for the job skills and competencies they can demonstrate.These systems also tend to mesh nicely with the changing nature of work and today's work environment. But the most critical factor is management's compensation philosophy.

Performance Appraisal and Management

It is important for managers to help their employees achieve the results expected.This is done through managing the performance of the employees the manager is responsible for.In managing performance, the manager identifies and communicates the expected performance standards and then evaluates or measures the performance against the standard.There are a variety of ways to assess a person's performance.

There are several ways in which managers can evaluate or measure the performance of their employees.

Written essays

That describe an employee's performance and suggestions for improvement require no complex forms or extensive training. But a good or bad appraisal may depend as much on the writing skill of a manager as on the actual performance of an employee.

With the *critical incidents* method, the appraiser writes down what an employee did that was especially productive or counterproductive. The key is to cite specific and key behaviours.

With graphic rating scales

Performance factors are listed such as quantity and quality of work, depth of knowledge, or initiative.The appraiser then rates each factor on an incremental scale.This method cannot provide the depth of information of essays or critical incidents, but it is less time consuming to develop and administer, and yields results that can be quantified.

Behaviourally anchored rating scales *BARS* combine the critical incidents and graphics rating scale approaches.The appraiser rates employees on items along a continuum.The points along the scale are examples of actual on-the-job behaviour rather than general descriptions or traits.

Multiperson comparisons

These are relative measuring devices.Group order ranking requires the rater to place employees into a particular classification, such as the top one-fifth. Individual ranking orders employees from best to worst.

Paired comparisons rank each employee with all other employees and rates each as either the weaker or superior member of the pair.

MBO assesses employees on how well they accomplish a specific set of objectives that have been determined to be critical in the successful completion of their jobs.Because MBO emphasizes ends rather than means, this method allows managers to choose the best path for achieving their goals.

A 360-degreereview seeks feedback for the person being rated from a variety of sources: such as peers, supervisors, and customers. Research shows that 360-degree appraisals offer more accurate feedback, empower employees, reduce subjective factors in evaluation, and develop leadership in an organization.

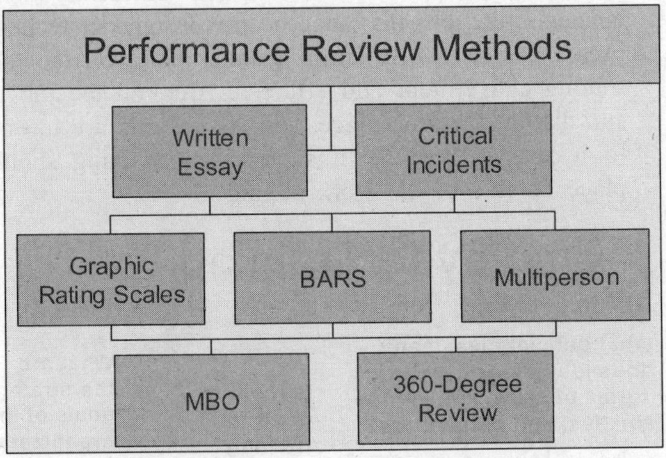

Training and Development

Training and development is important to ensure that people continue to learn skills, etc. to help the company be successful.Employee training is a learning experience that seeks a relatively permanent change in employees such that their ability to perform at their current job improves.This may mean changing what employees know, how they work, or their attitudes toward their jobs, co-workers, managers, and the organization.

- Management is responsible for deciding when employees are in need of training and development and what form it should take.
- Learning experience that seeks relatively permanent change
- Involves changing skills, knowledge, attitudes or behaviours
- Training tends to be done for current job
- Develop usually means acquiring skills for future work
- However, before any training takes place, and organization should determine is training is the appropriate intervention.
- Managers can be alerted to training needs by numerous signals: for instance, productivity related signals like decreases in output and quality or increases in accidents; and, future elements like jobs that have been redesignedor technological breakthroughs. Most Training takes place on the job. such traning conventent and effective. But, on the job training can disrupt the workplace, and some skills are too complex to learn on the job. In such cases, training should take place outside of the work setting.

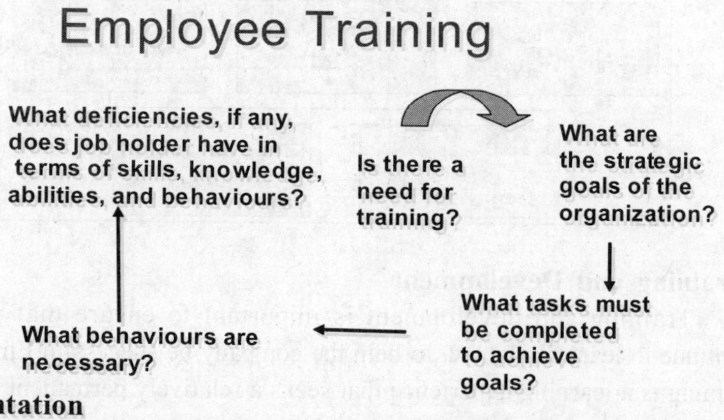

Orientation

Besides having the requisite knowledge,skills, and abilities to perform on the job, new hires must be socialized to the organization's culture (orientation) and trained to do the job (training).Orientation is a process whose major objectives are to reduce the anxiety level that all new employees feel; to familiarize them with the job, the work unit, and the organization; and to embed organizational values, beliefs, and accepted behaviours.

- Successful orientation maximizes new hire on-the-job success and minimizes turnover.
- Process to introduce new employees to organization.
- Familiarize new employee to job and work unit.
- Help employee to understand values, beliefs, and acceptable behaviours.

Specific Issues relating to Retailing

Human Resource Management is important for all organisation. However, in retailing, it has some specific and challenging issues for a number of reasons–

- Need for Part-Time Employees
- Demand on Expense Control
- Changing Employee Demographics
- Differing Cultural and Legal Requirements

Need for Part-Time Employees

Retailing needs diversified activities to satisfy the targeted customers having different types of needs.Here two factors become crucial one that there are some peak days and peak hours in a day when the number of customers visit is large. Similarly the shops/stores need to open for a longer hours particularly late in the night.Thus the same employees cannot render their services and store has to operate in atleast two shifts, therefore all employees are not recruited on regular basis and a large number of employees are employed as a part timers.The management of these part time employees is more difficult since mostly they are less committed and loyal to the organisation.The attrition rate is also much higher in their cases.It is estimated that about one third employees are engaged as part time workers.

Expense Control

Mostly the retailers operate on thin margin therefore they need to control the expenses rigorously to maintain their profit. Similarly, most of the jobs are unskilled or low skilled and therefore retailers take due precaution while paying wages to them. At times, they engage lower quality people, unskilled, inexperienced and less committed persons. Such persons are mostly those who are visible to customers and their total appearance, manners etc. results in negativity in terms of sales and profit.

Employee Demographics

The demographic pattern of a country has serious implications on the performance of retailers.In Western countries, e.g.,US, Europe etc. the growth in labour market is quite low hence there is chronic shortage of young energetic qualified persons in marketing. As against this, in India, the percentage of young people is high which results in unemployment and lower wages.Because of large number and lack of facilities, the large labour force is unskilled and lacks education.The values of aged and young are different The HRM needs to take in to account these features and adjust and accommodate variations.

Different culture and legal requirements

Since companies are functioning in a number of countries simultaneously, where the work values, system, labour land economic laws are different. A method of motivation or leadership may be effective in one but not in other.The legal and political and economic system of a country dictates the human resource management practices.

But what generates the better employee attitude at the start.

What are the qualities of a good team of employees in retail sector. These may be as given below–

- Experience
- Skills
- Motivated people
- Good management
- Strong direction –Teamwork

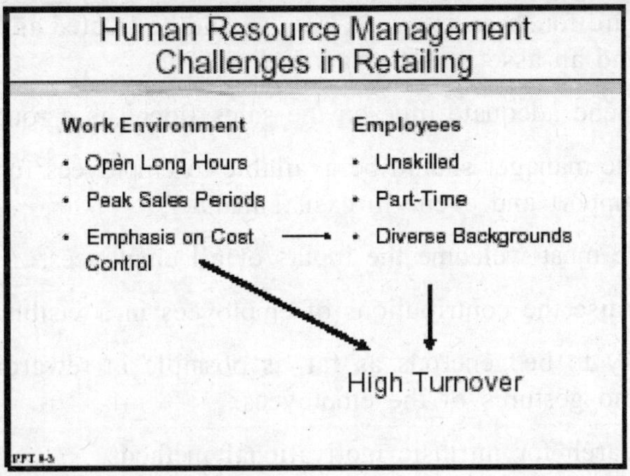

Motivating Retail Employees

One of the main function of Human Resource Management is to motivate workers toward achieving the organization's goal and implementing strategy effectively. Generally, following methods are used to retail employees-

- Written policies and procedures and its supervision
- Monetary and other incentives
- Development and induction of organization culture.

This motivation can be both Intrinsic and Extrinsic Motivation–

- Intrinsic (or Inner) Motivation causes people to participate in an activity for their own enjoyment. reward or to avoid a penalty. For example, kids play sports with their friends.
- Extrinsic (or External) Motivation – might enjoy the sport, but he/she causes people to do something for some external reward, remuneration.
- For example, a professional athlete chooses to play for a particular team because it pays more money or has more prestige.

There are a number of ways to motivate people. For retailers few guiding points are given below–

- Care for the employees.They should be treated as individuals and an asset to the organisation.
- Spend adequate time on the sales floor as a routine.
- The manager should be available to employees for guidance, support and even in casual manner..
- He must welcome the inputs of all employees.
- Praise the contributions of employees in a visible manner.
- Try to be generous as far as possible in rewarding efforts and gestures of the employees.
- Search for intrinsic motivational methods.

Building Employee Commitment

- Commitment and loyalty are two factors which ensure better performance in terms of customer satisfaction and therefore larger turnout and increased profitability. Lack of commitment results in high turnoverwhich adds to the cost and reduced performance.There can be various approaches to build commitment depending upon the nature of employees, situation and organisation itself, however some of major ones are Developing employee skills.
- Empowering employees.
- Creating partnership relationship.
- Opportunity for balancing careers and families.
- Flextime.
- Promotion from within.
- Legal and Ethical Issues in Managing Store Personnel.

A number of laws, regulations,ethical provisions influencing employment practices are made human resource management quite critical and challenging.The environment becomes quite complex and requires expertise in labour and others along with skill to guide and help other managers to comply with these provisions. Some of the issues are-

(a) Equal employment opportunity without any discrimination.

(b) Compensation and working hours.

(c) Labour relations- particularly provisions relating to Unions.

(d) Employee safety and health.

(e) Sexual harassment and gender considerations.

(f) Employee privacy.

(g) Fairness and distributive and procedural justice.

Questions:

1. Discuss the need of a so und organisation structure for retailing.
2. What is organisation design and what factors need to consider in developing the same?
3. Give atleast five objectives a small independent tool store should set when setting up its organisation structure.
4. What are the differences in setting up a retail organisation for small and large retailers?
5. What is the importance of Human Resource Management in retailing?
6. Would you organize functions differently for stores in the metro and the semi urban areas?
7. "The quality of store maintenance efforts affects consumer perception of the retailer, the life span of facilities, and operating expenses.Comment."
8. How you will motivate your employees in a retail general store?
9. Discuss scope of Human Resource Management.
10. Discuss- (a) Commitment of employees.

    (b) Recruitment.

    (c) Training and development.

CHAPTER 5

Store Location, Layout and Designing

Space is one of the most important infrastructure for a retail store. The process of management of a retail store starts with managing space. It is to be planned and determined how the various activities of retail operations are undertaken in the premises The main objectives of retail space management are:

(a) To obtain a high return on investment by increasing the productivity of retail space, which requires effective utilization of space for merchandise display and convenience of customers,

(b) To ensure a compatible, exciting and rational interface between the customer, merchandise and sales people.

Presently space is one of the most scarce thing in each country particularly where a retail store is established since it must be a place where shoppers could reach easily and frequently.The supply of space is fixed in the sense that it is not easy to expand either because of investment constraint or availability of the land. Managing space is the first and foremost concern of almost every retailer, when it comes to designing the store's interior.Space is always an expensive and scarce resource. Retailers always try to maximize the return on sales per square foot Allocation of the available space to departments, categories, various items and other purposes, is one of the most complicated and difficult decision before the retailer.Every retailer has to take decision on following issues, while managing the space:

(a) The nature and number of offerings, departments and suppliers.

(b) How to optimize the selling area and minimize the non-selling parts.? The selling area is that part where merchandise is presented and customers do actual shopping.The non-selling area consists of other activities and uses such as parking, entertainment,back area, staircases, circulation space, etc.

(c) What items, vendors, categories and departments are to be carried taking into account the space.?

(d) What should be the quantity of each item be carried at a time.?

(e) Where merchandise be located to get maximum attention and convenience to customer?

(f) The location and proportion of space allotted to different type of merchandise.

(g) How Security of the premises and items can be ensured and monitored without jeopardizing the profitability and look of the store?

The answers to these questions is not easy and require rational planning of the space.

Space Planning

Space planning systems can be split into two types – numeric and visual. Numeric planning systems simply allow users to take account of space available and to calculate ratios like return on space. Visual systems allow users to create 3 dimensional walk-through models of the stores and to preview the look of a store once ranging decisions have been made.

Store layout and visual merchandising are factors that contribute to the uniqueness of a store.The exterior and interior of a store convey several messages about the store to the consumers.The building that houses retail store, (whether new or old) and the exterior design of the store are important aspects of the design of the store.Marquees, walkways, entrances, doors, display windows, the height and size of the building, colors and materials used, and theft prevention are some of the key factors to be kept in mind while developing a store's exterior.

Planning a layout for the store's interior is the first step in designing the store's interior. Allocating space to various merchandise categories in a store is very important. Allocation of space can be based on many factors, like historical sales, gross margins, industry averages and strategic objectives. Apart from allocating space to various merchandise categories, space has to be allocated for carrying out some essential functions. Such space includes the back room for receiving the inventories and sorting them out, office and other functional spaces, aisles and customer service desks, floor space and wall space.The interior of a store influences the purchasing behaviour of the customers to a great extent. Designing the interior of a store in such a way as to influence customer behavior is referred to as visual merchandising. It includes optimum and appropriate use of fixtures, displays, color, lighting, music, scent, ceilings and floor, and designing all of these properly. Merchandise presentation is the most significant aspect of store design,because it helps attract customers' attention. A retailer can resort to many forms of presentation such as idea-oriented presentation, item-oriented presentation, price lining, colour presentation, vertical merchandising, tonnage merchandising and frontal presentation.

Prevention of losses due to merchandise pilferage is a major cause of concern for all retailers.This issue should be addressed at the initial stage of store design.The retailer can use many electronic security systems like CCTV and EAS for the prevention of such losses.Thus, by appropriately integrating the various elements of store design (both exterior and interior), a retailer can create an excellent image of itself in the target customer's mind.

Similarly cleanliness of store premises and maintenance of the store facade and the display windows,etc. are to be given equal importance and management of space is undertaken keeping these issues in mind.

Factors for Considerations in Space Management

The planning process always keep in mind the objectives in accordance with which various activities are organized. In general, the sales productivity is the main consideration of a retailer. Initially the store planner must adjust the estimate on the basis of the following:

(*a*) ***The degree of profitability of merchandise***: A retailer has to allocate space to stock keeping units to maximize the merchandise category's profitability.It is to be decided that whether popular brands be kept in forefront or other ones.The goods can be divided into 3 categories from this consideration–

- **(i)** **The staple goods** which are the core selling products of the store, and constitute nearly half of the store offering may be kept at the central and deeper ends of the store.This enhances visibility of all customers passing through the entire store to reach them. Shirts and trousers in a garment store or grains and sugar in a supermarket put in the category of staple goods.
- **(ii)** **Convenience goods** are no fuss basic merchandise and constitute about one third of the store and mostly bought in multiple units.Considering the convenience of customers they must be kept in a proper location where customer can find them immediately without any search.
- **(iii)** **Impulse purchase merchandise** has normally the highest rate of sale.The constitute about 15% of the total sales. These need to be given maximum exposure so that customers are tempted to buy them. Candies, socks,hair products, children games, etc. are some of such products. It is generally preferred to keep them near the cash counters and entrance.

Thus, locations of various goods are to be chosen carefully to ensure their exposures to customers for increasing profitability.

(b) ***Inventory turnover and the stock to sale ratio:*** In every retail store the monthly/daily inventory levels vary according to seasonal demands, holidays, festivals, etc.The space manager must allocate space on the basis of these seasonal needs rather than going by profitability or yearly averages.

(c) ***Displays and back up stock:*** Displays are very important to attract the attention of the customer whereas it occupies larger space as compared to back up stock in a storage area.

(d) ***Merchandise display:*** Fixtures and merchandise go together. Fixtures have a physical limitations and they occupy larger space,however products on them are more attractive.

(e) ***Importance to items:*** A retailer may wish to give greater importance to a item hence the space allocated to it should be prime one and displayed in a orderly manner.

(h) ***Size of items and space:*** Sometimes, retailer has to take a decision whether particular items, if they occupy large space, be continued to offer or dropped considering the cost effectiveness of the space.

(i) ***Personnel space:***The space is needed for use of personnel of the store for comforts, rests, coffee breaks, lunch, change clothes, etc.

(j) ***Customer space:*** In a big store, space for customers which include a lounge, benches, chairs, dressing rooms, a restaurant, a nursery, parking etc. influences customer and creates differentiations.

Approach

There are various types of approaches available to a retailer in the space management:

(a) **Top down** – He starts with its total available store space by dividing into categories and then works on product layouts.

(b) **Bottom up** – In this approach panning is undertaken at the individual product level and then proceed to the category, total store and overall organisation levels.

The space is management from other approach too–

(a) **Model stock method**–This approach determines the floor space necessary to carry and display a proper merchandise assortment.Generally, shoe and Apparel stores use this approach.

(b) **Sales productivity ratio**– It assigns floor space on the basis of sales or profit per foot.Those product categories which are highly profitable are allocated large chunks of space whereas marginally profitable categories get less. Book stores and food stores use this technique.

Another approach compares the performance of each activity with others in relation to space –

(a) **Hot Spot analysis**– This analysis identifies those areas where the off take of merchandise is the highest. Where merchandise sales are lower they are termed as warm spots and cold spots. The analysis is undertaken periodically and attempts are made to convert cold spots into warm and warm spots into hot sports.

The non treaded space where there is no customer traffic, is also identified.The black hole areas are also analyzed.

(b) **Efficiency analysis**– Efficiency of selling space to non-selling space is analysed.The utilization of selling and non-selling spaces-back area, facilities area, etc. are periodically monitored. A retailer always aims at optimizing selling space to improve the bottom line.However he takes care of efficiency of deliveries of the non- selling space.

Criterion to measure space performance:

The space performance can be judged by –

(i) **Sales per square foot** –This is also known as top line plan.This measures space productivity by volume of sale and value a received per square foot per day.

(ii) **Margins per square foot** – This is also called bottom line plan or gross margin return on footage. This measures the space productivity by gross margins earned per square foot per day.

(iii) Stock holding per square foot– This is also called bottom line tool or gross margin returns on inventory. It measures space productivity by the average inventory holding per square foot per day and compares with the ideal level of stock holding planned for a designated space in the store. Stock turns in such designated space plays vital role in earning good revenue returns on the space occupied when they are optimized.

The measurement of space performance is desired since it helps retailers in developing a blueprint for profitable deployment of space. It is more useful in chain store operations. The another advantage is that it also provide guidance for merchandise placing in the right locations to maximize profitability as well as uniformity for comfortable shopping by customers.

Certain guiding rules for space management:

(a) Convenience of the customer is the first thing – this is the golden rule of the retail floor space planning and management.

(b) Provide the maximum opportunity to the customer to walk around the store to enable him to browse through all the merchandise displayed.

(c) Optimize the trading space to achieve maximum sales however the significance of non trading area is not neglected. The customer should be kept engaged in the store for a long period.

(d) Since space cost is quite high, it is necessary that right floor space management decisions are made. Due analysis be made and corrective measures are taken on time.

(e) A retail floor need to be designed, planned and managed well from the point of target customer.The emotional connection with the buyer is established.The aesthetic and functionally effective ambience is developed.

Importance of planned space management:

The planned space management has several advantages.It is important from the point of view of both the retailer and customer.

(a) It enables a smooth and efficient customer flow not only into the store but within it.The other factors such as the fixtures, the placement of merchandise, floor arrangement, lay out and design all are directed toward the customer considerations.

(b) It provide the opportunity to the customer to reach and have access to desired merchandise without any inconvenience.

(c) The aesthetics of a well planned floor give an invitation to the customer where he would like to come time and again and develops a sense of belonging.

(d) A planned space management helps in creating a feeling of comfort in the minds of the customers. Generally, a large number of purchase decisions are made while walking on the floor of the store.

(e) Ultimately, it helps the retailer in selling more effectively and retain customers.

The planning of space calls planogram. A **Planogram** is a visual representation of the space for selling, merchandise, personnel, product categories,customers, including in store placement.Now a large number of retailers are using this for managing space.

STORE LOCATION

Retailing is the critical aspect of marketing.The most important P (Place) in retailing is the store location, i.e., at which place store is located. The location of any store in a most appropriate place is the first condition of success.The location of store conveys a fair amount of the image and influences the buying decision of the customer.Proper location many times is the guarantee of success and may compensate some of the negative features.

The scarcity of land at a proper place is responsible for high price and rent of the property.The decision to start a new store is determined to a great extent by the availability of property at a proper location.

In India, the emergence of organized retailing is facing the problem of location since the property in desired size, type and related infrastructure is not available at suitable location.

Significance of location:

Where a retailer chooses to locate his retail business will have a major impact on everything that shop does. The difference between selecting the wrong location and the right site could be the difference between business failure and success. The location decision is likely to answer of these three questions–

- Where to place a market
- How to estimate sales
- How to factor in competition
- How many customers will come to the store?
- Where should we locate our store?
- What kind of store will work?

Thus, Store location is the most important decision before a retailer for a number of reasons–

- It involves a large capital investment since the property is to be located at an appropriate place which might be considered prime location from various considerations.
- The location is to be decided in keeping in mind the convenience of target customers.
- Location decision will be determined by the nature of merchandize since a customer will take decision regarding traveling a particular distance on the basis of nature of product or service. Since it adds to the cost of transportation and time consumed.
- The customer always prefer a store closest to home, locality, work place. Thus it affects the amount of customer traffic.

- The location decision has a strategic importance since it may provide in developing a sustainable competitive advantage.
- It is difficult to change the location in a short period and even in a long period without bearing extra cost. The retailer can change his merchandise mix, adjust prices, improve communication with consumers and change the services officered but once a store comes into existence, it is quite difficult to change location. Changing location means loosing image, customers, employees and incur huge cost. Location decisions are harder to change because retailers have to make huge investment in buying, developing and designing the layouts, etc according to his needs. Normally he has to acquire the property on long term leases.
- The competition among the retailers make the decision of location difficult and costly since various big retailers are opening new locations.The problem becomes acute when there is slowdown both in population growth and construction of new shopping centres.
- Location is the major factor in determining the volume of business and thereby the revenue of the store.
- The high rent, complicated leases and expensive fixturing and remodeling etc. can increase the cost and therefore need proper attention.

In fact, organized retail is related to cities. Actually What are cities? They are the centres which provide

- Employment
- Shopping
- Social centers
- Private property
- Public amenities
- And primary shopping centres make them grow.

Types of Retail locations

There are a number of types of retail location available which a retailer can have

The Isolated Store

The isolated store is that where there are no other outlets available in the vicinity of the store.This is also called Free standing locations since it depends upon its own power and quality to attract the customers.

Such a store is located along a major traffic route having no other competitor around it. Such a store has several advantages–

(a) Absence of any competitor in close proximity.

(b) Rents are usually low.

(c) Flexibility in operation since no group rules need to be followed.

(d) Larger space is available for operation as well as parking, etc.

(e) Better road and traffic visibility is possible.

(f) Facilities can be adapted to individual specifications.

(g) Possibility of cost reduction is there.

(h) The element of monopoly helps in increasing revenue.

However it has several disadvantages too-

(a) It may be difficult to attract customers initially.

(b) People may not like to travel very fare to get something unless they have to pass through that way.

(c) Most people like variety in shopping.

(d) Advertisement expenditure may be high

(e) Additional costs such as outside lighting, security, are to be incurred since no external economies are available.

(f) A store must often be built rather than rented thus higher capital expenditure is required.

(g) Urban bodies zoning laws may restrict access to desirable locations.

(h) Generally planned shopping centers are preferred by the consumers.

(i) The customer will avoid additional travel cost particularly when it is at a distance.

Neighbourhood stores

Stores which are located in residential neighbourhoods to serve the small locality are known as neighbourhood stores.Generally, they sell convenience products.Such stores operate on a lower scale and may charge higher price even.

* **Part of a Business district**

A retail store can be located as a part of a business districti, e., a place of commerce in a city which has developed as the centre of trade commerce historically. Mostly, it is unplanned and has no pre-set format or structure. Such a centre could be –

(i) Central

(ii) Secondary

(iii) Neighbourhood

The Central business district is the main centre of commerce and trade in the city. It is hub of retailing activity in a city. It has the trade area that varies according to the size of the city.In big cities like Delhi or Bombay customers even from suburbs come for shopping. It has good accessibility in terms of transport from all the parts of the city. Being part of such a business district has its own advantages and disadvantages.The retailer is not required to spend any additional amount for drawing customers however the rents may be high and space may not be available for facilities like parking.

The Central Business District has certain strength for which it is preferred by the customers.

(a) Excellent goods/service assortment.

(b) Having variety of store types and positioning strategies within the area.

(c) Range of prices may be large.

(d) Variety of customer services.

(e) Access to public transportation.

(f) Pedestrian traffic is large.

(g) Nearness to commercial and social facilities and the people may visit the area even having no intention to make purchases.

However there are number of weaknesses too–

(a) Lack of planned development of the Centre.

(b) Inadequate services such as parking, conveyance.

(c) Traffic and delivery congestion.

(d) Longer travel time for those living in the suburbs.

(e) Few stores may be old and traditional.

(f) Relatively poor image of some potential customers.

(g) High rents and taxes for the most popular sites.

(h) Space shortage for assortment.

The Secondary business district is one which has evolved over a period of time as a result of increase in population of the city.The number of such centers can be more than one.They attract customers from a large part of the city. A large number of retail stores may be located here however the size may be smaller than the Central Business District.

The neighbourhood business district is one which has emerged as a shopping area to serve the needs of the nearby locality and in not planned. A number of retailers small in size may be established here.

Part of a Shopping Centre

Shopping center has been defined by the International Council of Shopping Centers as"a group of retail and other commercial establishments that is planned, developed, owned and managed as a single property." It is planned shopping center which consists of a group of architecturally unified commercial establishments on a site that is centrally owned or managed, designed and operated as a unit.Its location, size and mix of stores are related to the trading area which it serves.The quality,variety of products etc.are determined by the needs of the population.The parking facility is an important feature.To maintain the balance various product lines are allocated space in a reasonable manner.

It has several advantages–

(a) Well planned assortments of goods and services keeping in mind the long range operation.

(b) Customers are mainly from sub urban areas.

(c) A centre for family shopping since it is only one stop shopping.

(d) Advantageous to retailers since common costs are shared.

(e) Unified distinctive image of shopping centre.

(f) Pedestrian traffics is maximized for individual store.

(g) Access to highways and available of adequate parking facility.

(h) More spacious hence more appealing than city shopping for a number of customers.

(i) Generally rents and taxes are lower

(j) Growth of discount malls and competitive prices.

(k) Availability of many services including entertainment, controlled temperature and demonstration of even large size products.

Inspite of these, there maybe some limitations of such centers-

(a) Rent may be high as compared to isolated store.

(b) A highly competitive environment within the centre.

(c) Regulations by the landlord may reduce the flexibility of retailer.

(d) Sometimes there are restrictions on the goods/services that can be sold by each store.

(e) Extra payments for certain common purposes which may not be revenue earning to retailer such as membership of the merchants' association.

(f) The number of malls may be large in a area.

(g) Domination by large anchor stores.

These shopping centers are quite important.According to the International Council of Shopping Centers, there are 48000 US shopping centers about 1130 of which are fully enclosed shopping malls.In India, Cannaught Place was developed initially as a shopping Center.Now a large number of cities are having such Centers.

During the course of time, the retail markets in the West have brought a various shopping centre formats.The International Council of Shopping Centers has defined 8 types of shopping centers–

- Neighbourhood shopping Centre.
- Community shopping Centre.
- Regional Shopping Centre.
- Super Regional Centre
- Fashion/Specialty Centre
- Power Centre
- Theme Centre
- Outlet Centre.

In India, a different type of markets are found which may be termed as **Periodic Markets.**

Periodic Market

Such markets are organized at a particular place on particular days during a week. Such markets are generally operate during evening and serve lower and middle class families.These are very popular where there is high concentration of population particularly of a given income level.They provide large number of products.The shops are arranged on a temporary basis for certain hours and a nominal rent is paid to the local government.

The major features of various types of shopping centers are given below to have a comparison at a glance.

Types of Shopping Centers

Name	Radius	Building Area	Parking area
Convenience/ Neighborhood	6 min.	30-100 KSF	Nil
Community	15 min.	100-500 KSF	Negligible
Regional	30+ min	500-1,000 KSF	Limited
Super-Regional	45 min.	>1,000,000 SF	Adequate

Factors Affecting Store Location

While starting a retail store every retailer witnesses a important question – where to locate the store?The question is to be answered from two dimensions.

– Where is the best location to put a new store?

– Is the location of my present store (s) most effective?

Evaluating an existing store

✦ Local store marketing plan versus local geography

✦ What is the trade area?

- ✦ What are distribution networks of the retailer?
- ✦ Where are the competitors? Are there any new competitors?
- ✦ Is the store local service or traffic oriented or both
- ✦ What are the forecasting models?
  - – Demographic data ... changing population
  - – Traffic count data
  - – Drive times to the store
- ✦ Simple maps of trade areas that could be about 1mile radius
- ✦ Locate all competitors
- ✦ Evaluate locations of growth in the local markets
- ✦ What more could they do?
  - – Travel distances to all stores including competitors
  - – Location of potential special incentive programs – schools etc.

Evaluating a new store

- **Store Prospecting**
  - – Searching for new sites for your business
  - – Define store-based trade areas for a new store

Customer Market Analysis

- – Defined by distance customers travel to stores
- – Calculate market penetration
- – Locate untapped markets
- – Assumes you know the location of your customers

Customer Prospecting

- – Create profiles of existing customers
- – Then look for areas with similar profiles

Store Market Analysis

– Assumes you do not know where the customers live

– Store-based trade areas

- ✦ Simple rings
- ✦ Data driven rings
- ✦ Equal competition areas
- ✦ Drive time areas along street networks
- ✦ Locational questions …

– **Do the targeted customers live, work or play near my site?**

– **Which customer segments are driving the business?**

– **How far are the customers willing to travel to shop?**

– **Is the site well placed to defend or dominate a market?**

– **How can retailer increase trade area traffic?**

– **What is the best venue/store mix for a site?**

– **Where should locate a site relative to existing locations?**

Location Costs

Besides the base rent, consider all costs involved when choosing a retail store location.

- ✦ Who pays for lawn care, building maintenance, utilities and security?
- ✦ Who pays for the upkeep and repair of the heating/air units?
- ✦ If the location is remote, how much additional marketing will it take for customers to find the store?
- ✦ How much is the average utility bill?

- Will itneed to make any repairs, do any painting or remodeling to have the location fit your needs?
- Will the retailer be responsible for property taxes?

The location retailer can afford now and what he can afford in the future should vary. It is difficult to create sales projects on a new business, but one way to get help in determining how much rent he can pay is to find out what sales similar retail businesses are making and how much rent they're paying.

Personal Factors

While planning on store location, retailer must think about his personality, the distance from the shop to home and other personal considerations. If he spends much of his time travelling to and from work, the commute may overshadow the exhilaration of being his own boss. Also, many restrictions placed on a tenant by a landlord, management company or community can hamper a retailer's independence.

Special Considerations

The retail shop may require special considerations.A list of any unique characteristic be made of the business that may need to be addressed.

- Will the store require special lighting, fixtures or other hardware installed?
- Are restrooms for staff and customers available?
- Is there adequate fire and police protection for the area?
- Is there sanitation service available?
- Does the parking lot and building exterior have adequate lighting?
- Does the building have a canopy that provides shelter if raining?
- What is the crime rate in the area?

- ✦ Are there restrictions on Sunday/any other specific day sales?

A retailer need not feel rushed into making a decision on where to put the retail store.Take adequate time, research the area and have patience. If necessary be prepared to change the schedule and push back the date of the store's opening, than do so.Waiting to find the perfect store location is better than just settling for the first place that comes along. The wrong location choice could be devastating to retail business.

What consumers see of any retail environment is initially visual.That why the key to a store's marketing strategy is its identity and image. Strategic identity is a strong concept developed early on in the marketing positioning process,whether it's a new store or repositioning of an existing one.

How to choose retail location?

Choosing a right site and location is a very strategic decision for a retailer.Once a location is chosen, it is desirable that a retailer must live with that for a longer period.It is to be understood clearly that selection of appropriate site is one of the most critical thing since even if a retailer finds the right neighbourhood, the wrong site can spell disaster.Here, he has to identify 3 levels–

(a) Regional Analysis – keeping in mind the degree of demand.

(b) Trade area analysis – A trade areas is the geographic area that generates the majority of the customers for the store..

(c) Site selection – that exact area where the store is to be located where the targeted customers can be attracted.

Retailers desire to set up their outlets in the best possible locations. The optimum store location for a retailer is based on many factors like the type of industry, the product category being sold, and the degree of competition. Retail stores are located where the opportunities offered by the market are at a maximum.

From the above considerations following steps are suggested as a procedure.

(1) Market identification

The retailer's first concern is the market where the customers can be attracted to visit the store.Various theories are available in assessing the attractiveness of a market.

(2) Assessing the market potential

Assessment of market potential is equally important for a retailer since that will only determine the success of the store. A number of factions are considered in determining the market potential

(3) Demographic features – of the population

The size, nature, age, growth rate etc.are to be assessed. Researching some of the following information is necessary.

- What neighbourhoods are home to your target market?
- How far will prospective customers travel to shop at your location?
- What are the statistical trends in a proposed location, i.e. population growth; aging trends, etc? How might this affect your store 5 or 10 years after locating?

What are the employee demographics in particular areas?With labour shortages becoming an ongoing challenge for retailers, does your proposed location have access to potential full time and part-time employees.

(4) Households characteristics.

The economic and social factors are to be known in advance.The income category, income growth are more important.The nature of product mix will be determined on the basis of this.

Competition and compatibility– It is to be identified that what is degree of competition and whether the retail store is compatible with others or not? On this basis a restaurant is located near shopping centres, cinema theater etc. However, a fashion garment store may not be a ideal location nearby a bakery or antique shop.

Laws and regulations- Which govern the establishment, operation and products, traffic etc.are to taken into account since violation of any such provision may cause serious harm to store in future.Some things to consider are:

- ✦ **Zoning** – Are there any restrictions that might prevent a retailer from doing specific renovations or leasehold improvements?
- ✦ **By-Laws** – What are some of the laws that might have an affect of retail operation? For example, Whether retailer is able to use the space in front of his store for promotions...or he is restricted from operating during certain hours, etc?
- ✦ **Planning** – Are there any major development plans that could impact retailer's operation? Is there any major road construction planned close to his store?

Traffic – The vehicular and pedestrian traffic that passes the site is an important determinant of the potential sales of the store.There should be compatibility between traffic and products of the store.It's also important to know how vehicle and pedestrian traffic patterns might affect business at a proposed location. Some things to look for include:

- ❒ Access to the store by traffic moving in both directions (both by car and on foot).
- ❒ Number of cars passing the store location.
- ❒ Number of pedestrians walking by the location.
- ❒ Proximity to public transit.

Accessibility of the market – The availability of efficient and cheap transport- both public and private is an essential condition for the success of a store.

The total number and type of stores in the area – A trade area having a large number of stores is normally attracting large number of customers.The type of stores is equally important since if market is having large number of stores of a particular product then an altogether different product store may not be successful, e.g., in a hardware market a cloth store is likely to be a failure.

Availability of amenities – Depending upon the nature of store, the level and nature of amenities need to be considered seriously.

The Competitors- The number and type of competitors are equally important. A retailer must have thorough knowledge of all the competitors in a proposed location.

For some retailers locating near the competition makes sense because having similar businesses located near one another may increase traffic flow. This strategy is known as clustering and works well for products where customers are likely to comparison shop.

Overcrowding businesses of the same type in an area can create an undesirable impact on the profitability of all competing firms.Lack of competition may have merit in certain situations.

Thus competitors can be termed as good and bad

Bad competitors are those that will have a negative effect on his business. Some examples might include retail stores that might be selling the exact same products (at a discount) or stores that attract the opposite target audience as his retail operation.

Good competitors are retail stores that compliment his business by drawing a similar target audience to his store's surrounding area. A good example are retail "pockets"that exist in many cities–shopping destinations that attract larger numbers of consumers by offering complimentary stores in close proximity to one and other, i.e., fashion districts, areas with a high concentration of art galleries, auto malls, etc.

Product mix-The product mix will have an impact on such things as the amount of square footage and storage space required at the location. If it is a service provider, factors such as office space will be an important consideration.The choice of location is also influenced by the product mix offered.A supermarket need to be located near residential area whereas a entertaining cum dine plaza can be located slightly away from the residential area.

STORE LAYOUT AND DESIGN

An industry experts observed that "a shopper should be able to determine the following about a store in three seconds; its name, its line of trade, its claim to fame, its price positions and its personality."This requires developing a distinct image of the store in which its design and layout plays a vital role.A well-planned retail store layout allows a retailer to maximize the sales for each square foot of the allocated selling space within the store. Store layouts generally show the size and location of each department, any permanent structures,fixture locations and customer traffic patterns. Each floor plan and store layout will depend on the type of products sold, the building location and how much the business can afford to put into the overall store design.

A retailer must plan store layout, atmosphere, and create irresistible visual merchandising displays.He needs to view floor plans and other retail store designs. He must learn how to select and care for store fixtures, as well as using special lighting techniques to accent his products. He should find store layout software and browse his resource of vendors selling store fixtures and displays.

The purpose of designing store layout is quite clear that customer is attracted to enter the store and once entered in the store he is motivated silently to visit the entire store offering.The entrance creates expectations and contains promises. Customers need to be led on a journey throughout the store.This is achieved by planning the circulation and location of the merchandise. While designing store layout, generally circulation planning is done to lead the customer from area to area with the help of aisles that weave through the merchandise area. With the help of accent lighting and displays strategically placed the focal points are highlighted.The width of the aisles is planned according to the density and traffic pattern.

TYPES OF STORE LAYOUTS

The specifics of store layout re sequentially planned and enacted. It requires floor planning in such a way that fulfills the objectives of retailer.There are following basic retail floor plan:

1. Straight Floor Plan
2. Diagonal Floor Plan
3. Angular Floor Plan
4. Geometric Floor Plan
5. Mixed Floor Plan

Straight Floor Plan

Straight Floor Plan

The straight floor plan is an excellent store layout for most any

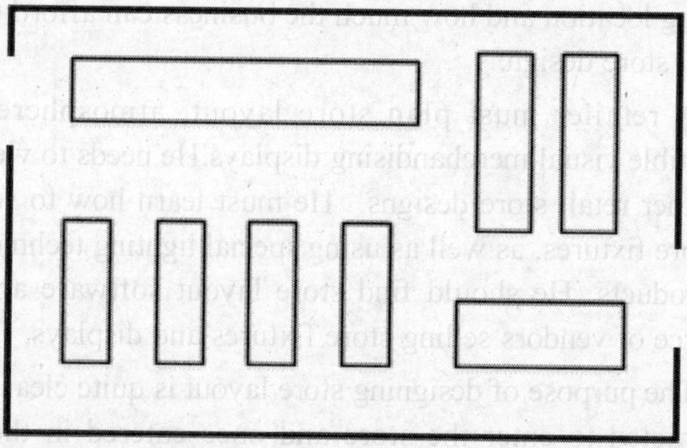

type of retail store.It makes use of the walls and fixtures to create small spaces within the retail store.The straight floor plan is one of the most economical store designs. It takes into consideration the traffic flow.It places displays and aisles in a rectangular or grid iron pattern.

Diagonal Floor Plan

Diagonal Floor Plan

Sponsored Links

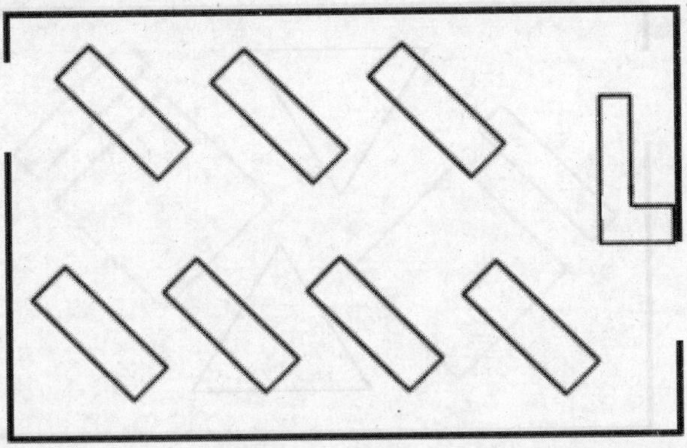

The diagonal floor plan is a good store layout for self-service types of retail stores.It offers excellent visibility for cashiers and customers. The diagonal floor plan invites movement and traffic flow to the retail store.

Angular Floor Plan

Angular Floor Plan

The angular floor plan is best used for high-end specialty stores.

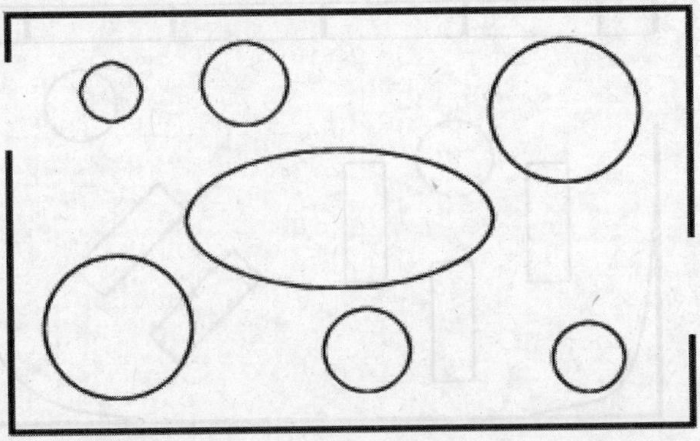

The curves and angles of fixtures and walls makes for a more expensive store design.However,the soft angles create better traffic flow throughout the retail store.

Geometric Floor Plan

Geometric Floor Plan

Sponsored Links

The geometric floor plan is a suitable store design for clothing and apparel shops.It uses racks and fixtures to create an interesting and out-of-the-ordinary type of store design without a high cost.

Mixed Floor Plan

Mixed Floor Plan

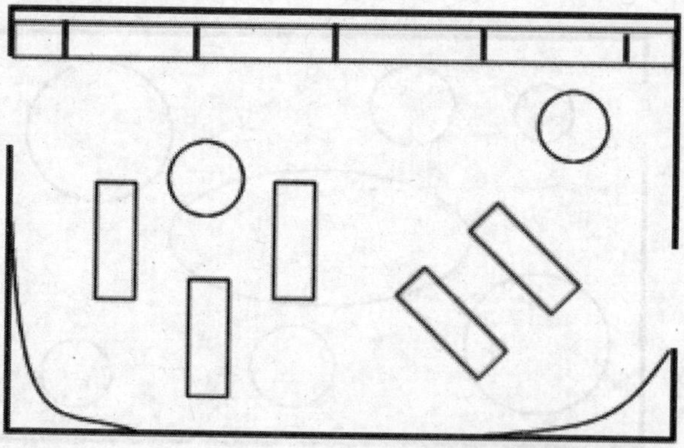

The mixed floor plan incorporates the straight, diagonal and angular floor plans to create the most functional store design.The layout moves traffic towards the walls and back of the store.

Designing

The design and layout are the integral part of retailing.

The designing of a store layout and appearance is one of the most important factor determining the sales, image and customer satisfaction.The physical appearance of the building provides customers with their first impression of a business and contributes significantly to establishing its identity in the customer's mind. New businesses should plan their space requirements one to two years ahead and update the estimates every six months.

As retailers move into the realm of **designing** a customer oriented environments,three critical elements of ***commerce,content and community*** must be addressed in order to build and facilitate customer relationships.

OBJECTIVES OF A GOOD STORE DESIGN

✦ **Design should be consistent with Image and strategy:**The retailer must determine the target customers land their needs while designing a store.

✦ **Design should be consistent with the life style and culture of the people:**It must be remembered that customers are guided by their culture and behave mostly according to their life style.

✦ **Design should influence consumer behaviour.**The consumer behaviour is influenced both positively and negatively by the total environment of store.Care has to be taken so that no negative signal is communicated influencing the behaviour of consumer.

✦ **Considering costs versus value:**The retailer must consider the costs associated with each store design element versus the value received in terms of higher sales and profits. A retailer must develop the planograms that prescribe the location of merchandise based on profitability and other factors.

✦ **Design should be flexible :**The design should be such that has maximum flexibility. This flexibility can be of two types – one the ability to physically move store components and second, the ease with which components can be modified.Earlier, this factor was not given importance, however now most stores are designed with keeping in mind the desired flexibility.

Design should encourage customers to spend more time shopping: Longer the period a customer stays in store higher purchases he is likely to make.The amount of time a shopper spends in a store is the single most important factor in determining the amount of purchases.

Types of Design

The retailers are using various types of design.The major ones are:

✦ **Grid :**Grid design is typically used in a supermarket where the aisles and fixtures are at right angles to each other.Most grocery and drug store operations are having this design.Although grid is not the most aesthetically pleasuring arrangement,still it is very good for shopping trips in which customers need to move throughout the entire store and easily locate products.This saves the time of the customer and is cost effective to retailer.The merchandise on the floor can be significantly more than with other layouts.

✦ **Racetrack :** This is used in larger and wider stores where the customer is made to circle around the flow and get back to the beginning, usually the lift or the staircase lobby, to move to the next level of the store. It is also known as a loop. It provides a major aisle to facilitate customer traffic, with access to the store's multiple entrances.The problem with the grid design is that customer is not exposed to all of the merchandise in the store unless he is clear in the mind that what he is going to buy. The design should be such that pull customer through store that want to encourage them to explore and seek out new and interesting merchandise.The racetrack design encourages impulse purchasing since as the customer goes around the racetrack, his eyes are forced to take different viewing angles.

✦ **Free Form:** It is successfully used primarily in small specialty stores or within the departments of large stores particularly where the merchandise and fixtures are grouped in clusters.This provides a relaxed environment and a customer feel that he is at someone's home rather than in a store.This facilitates and encourages shopping.However, this is more expensive since such an atmosphere creation requires additional expenditure. Moreover it is difficult for sales persons to keep watch on adjacent departments, there is greater possibility of theft. Similarly, some additional space is required to create spacious environment for the customer. Nevertheless, if properly designed, such layout increases the sales and the profit margin.

✦ **Herringhone circulation** – Such lay out is used for a narrow store jparticularly where the highway is a single two way one.There are side roads leading to the walls from it.If side roads are not there, it is called the **Spine form**.

Besides these designs, there are a number of issues which are related with designing.

Feature Area –These are the areas within a store designed to get the customer's attention.These are the part of promotional activity. Some of these are given here –

End Caps –These are displays located at the end of an aisle to catch consumer attention. One can notice a large end cap display of Cold Drink or any food item. It is the high visibility that is used to feature special promotion.

Promotional area–The area which is used to display merchandise that is being promoted particularly of seasonal merchandise. Lawns or open space is decorated and lighted during Diwali and other festival.The merchandise is often placed in the back.

Windows: Windows are external to the store yet they form an important component of the store layout.Window displays help in drawing customers into the store provided they are properly used. A visual message is provided through these windows about the type of merchandise for sale in the store and the type of image the store wishes to convey.

Walls: Since the space is scare and expensive walls are used to display merchandise and creatively present a message by proper design. It suits and catches the eyes of customer since he feels comfortable with larger space to move.Overall the designing layout should take into consideration following to achieve the goal of larger sales and profit margin.

✦ **Size:** A building must be large enough to accommodate a business's daily operations comfortably. For example, there should be an area inside the front door that is void of product display.This area of perhaps 12 or 14 feet square has been termed the "decompression zone". The decompression zone allows customers to enter your store and adjust to your environment.The decompression zone,when done right, communicates a "welcome" to your patrons and allows them to make their first judgements of your retail world.

✦ ***Construction & External Appearance***: It pays to have an expert look it over before buying or leasing the property.Recognize the importance of creating the proper image for their store and how their shop's layout and physical facility influence this image.The appearance should reflect the business's personality. Externally the store front, its architectural style and colour, signs, entrances and general appearance give important clues to customers about the business's image. A glass front enables a retail business to display merchandise easily and to attract potential customers' attention.

✦ **Entrances**: All entrances to a business should invite customers in. Wide entry ways and attractive merchandise displays that are set back from the doorway can draw customers into a business.Underhill has observed that is what he has named the "invariant right". This refers to the fact that when given the opportunity people prefer to, and most often do, move to the right after entering a store. stores should take a lesson from the culture and create store layouts that facilitate a quick traverse.

✦ **Balance and Symmetry**: A couple of additional store layout basics that I consider are balance and symmetry.Most people react positively to both balance and symmetry. the shopping war is one by stores that "feel better" to their patrons.Never forget how important retail store layouts are to the feel of a store.(1)

(1) Philip H. Mitchell is the author of Discovery-Based Retail.

✦ ***Signs:*** One of the lowest cost and most effective methods of communicating with customers is a business sign. Signs should be large enough for people passing by to read.Contrasting colours and simple type faces are best. Therefore always check for sign ordinances.There should be co-ordination between signs and graphics with the store's image. Informative signs and graphics make merchandise more desirable The signs and graphics should be used as props.It is a great wail to unify a theme and merchandise for an appealing overall presentation.The signs and graphics should look fresh.They should be relevant to the items displayed and should never the left in the store or in windows after displays are removed. Irrelevant, forgotten, faded and having water spots signs do more harm than sell merchandise. Signs can also be used to create theatrical effects.It is necessary that appropriate typefaces are used since different typefaces impart different messages and moods

Interiors: Designing a functional,efficient interior is important. Ergonomics is the science of adapting work and the work environment to complement employee's strengths to suit customer's needs (helps employees perform the job more productively).This process should reduce accidents, injuries, and absenteeism and increase productivity and morale. It can also increase store traffic and boost sales and profits.

* **Proper lighting:** It is measured by what is ideal for the job being done. Lighting is usually an inexpensive investment.The use of natural and artificial light in combination can give a business an open and cheerful look.The appropriate lighting is positively influence customer shopping behaviour.A good lighting system helps creates a sense of excitement in the store.

* The lighting is used to highlight merchandise.The lighting is also used for popping the merchandise, i.e., focusing spotlights on special feature areas and items.Lighting, music and decor determined by the type of department.

Music: Like lighting and colour, music too can attract or detract customer from a retail store.

* **Scent:** Many buying decisions are based on emotions rather than need and rationality.The fragrance has a deep impact on our emotions.It influences feelings of happiness,hunger, disgust and nostalgia.The marketers can take advantage of this.

✦ **Building:** The look and design of building has immense effect on customer. Timely renovation may help retailer in increasing the sale. It has–

✦ Advantages: Business looks new, creates a modern image, efficient, top quality, by using up to date equipment can lower operating costs.

✦ Disadvantages: High initial fixed costs, require more time and money.

✦ Decision to Buy a new building has also several advantages.It allows for remodeling without seeking permission, payment for facility is fixed. However the disadvantages like limits mobility, expensive are also lthere.

Displays: Retailers are putting more emphasis on the display of merchandise to attract consumers because there are so many alternatives for shopping, such as e-commerce and catalogues "Displays change on an ongoing basis, yet the emphasis remains the same: Make the store easier to shop and persuasive enough to get the customers to buy. Some issues are–

✦ "Give the Lady What She Wants"

"Attract Children as early as possible"

"Provide comforts to customer"

"Men's only on Second Floor"

"Children only on III Floor"

"Women's on Fourth & Fifth Floor"

"All have accessories on First Floor"

The retailer should start brainstorming or "white-boarding" ideas of what his target audience might expect when they enter the store.It is suggested that make a list of all the factors one can think of including display space, # aisles, aisle width, shipping/receiving area, storage space, office space, in-store traffic flow, etc. Once he is able to visualize what the shopping experience looks like for his customer, he will gain a better idea of what will be required in a location.

Good outlay

- ★ Crowded
- ★ Stocked like a department store
- ★ Primary displays, few secondary displays
- ★ Lots of racks
- ★ Hectic, congested transportation between floors

Main Level

- ★ Cosmetics
- ★ Women's Shoes

Second Level

- ★ Men's Merchandise

Third Level

Women's Apparel

High-end designer lines

Classic or Conservative Collections

Wood trim

Modern Collections

Vibrant colours

Lighting displays

Poor Layout

2 Floors

First Floor

Accessories

Cosmetics

All were very small

Felt like a cheap, crowded department store

Light music in background

Store signs looked cheap

Plain mannequins

No makeup

No faces

Racks overflowing

Avoid

The experience suggests that one common problems are illegible, poorly designed, properly located, poorly maintained, and have colour schemes that are unattractive or hard to read.Therefore, avoid–

Outdated, dull look

Poor Lighting

Felt like a retirement home

Brands had their own alcove

Limited inventory on floor

Soft music

Dull show

Cold environment

Ignored customers based on financial status

Desirable Layout

Easy to read map

Very Spacious

Customer Friendly Shopping Environment

Comfortable Chairs

Clean displays to accent special items

Add home décor to give display style

Racks are not stuffed full

Information

Easy Access

Accessible to information

Emails about sales

Shopping online under construction

Online accounts

Latest trends

Easy shopping categories

E-mails about fashion and sales

Special Services

Credit Card

Rewards

Personal Shoppers

Gift/Bridal Services

Weekly Advertisement

Personnel

Trained employees

Store was overwhelming with smiley, attractive faces

Friendly

Helpful

Empowered

Questions

1. What are the factors that a retailer needs to take into account while choosing a location for a retail store?
2. How do facilities like adequate parking and easy access to public transportation affect the developments of shopping areas?
3. Discuss the impact of high real estate costs and the general unavailability of large sites in metropolitan areas, on the retail industry in India.
4. Discuss the developments in the retail properties of India. What are the problems that are likely to arise due to the rapid and unplanned development?
5. How a retail food store increase the size of its trading area?
6. "A good location may let a retailer succeed event if its strategy mix is mediocre." Is it always true? Give examples.
7. Discuss characteristics of good and poor location.What a retailer should avoid?
8. What considerations a retailer have in designing layout to achieve the goal of larger sales and profit margin?
9. Discuss various types of design layout in retailing.
10. How to evaluate an existing and a new store location?

References -

1. A Gunasekaran, C Patel, E Tirtiroglu (2001). "Performance measures and metrics in a supply chain environment."*International Journalof Operations & Production Management,* Volume 21, Number 1, Page 71 - 87.

2. Alan G Hallsworth, Steve Worthington (2000). "Local resistance to larger retailers:the example of market towns and the food superstore."*International Journal of Retail & Distribution Management,* Volume 28, Number 4, Page 207- 216.

3. Alan C McKinnon (1992). "Retail Supply Chain Electronic Data Interchange: TheDistribution Contractor's Role."*Logistics Information Management,* Volume 5, Number 2, Page 165 - 172.

4. Arthur Meidan, Anne Tomes (1993). "Cash And Carry Customers." Shopping Habits and Supplier choice criteria." *International Journal of Retail & Distribution Management,* Volume 19, Number 5, Page 122 -126.

5. Angela da Rocha, Luis Antonio Dib (2002). "The entry of Wal-Mart in Brazil and the competitive responses of multinational and domestic firms." *International Journal of Retail & Distribution Management,* Volume 30, Number:1, Page 61 - 73.

6. Astad Pastakia (1998). "Grassroots ecopreneurs: change agents for a sustainable society." *Journal of Organizational Change Management,* Volume 11, Number 2 Page: 157- 173.

7. B Andries, L Gelders (1995). "Time-based manufacturing logistics." *Logistics Information Management,* Volume 8, Number 3, Page 30 - 36.

8. Benita M Beamon (1999). "Measuring supply chain performance." *International Journal of Operations & Production Management,* Volume 19, Number 3, Page 275- 292.

9. Beverly K Brockman, Robert M Morgan (1999). "The evolution of managerial innovations in distribution: what prospects for ECR?" *International Journal of Retail & Distribution Management,* Volume 27, Number 10, Page: 397 - 408.

10. Biren Prasad (1995). "JIT quality matrices for strategic planning and implementation." *International Journal of Operations & Production Management,* Volume 15, Number 9, Page 116 -141.

11. CII – Mckinsey (2004). "Indian Retail Environment." Page 21- 42-52

12. C Anthony Di Benedetto, Roger J Calantone, Chun Zhang (2003). "International technology transfer: Model and exploratory study in the People's Republic of China." *International Marketing Review*, Volume 20, Number 4, Page 446 - 462.

13. Carlos Melo Brito (2001). "Towards an institutional theory of the dynamics of industrial networks." *Journal of Business and Industrial Marketing,* Volume 16, Number 3, Page: 150 - 166.

14. Charles X Wang (2002). "A general framework of supply chain contract models." *Supply Chain Management: An International Journal*, Volume: 7 Number: 5 Page: 302 - 310.

15. Christopher Rau (2003). "Are you getting value from your IT?." *Journal of Business Strategy,*Volume: 24 Number: 3 , Page: 16 - 20.

16. Cliff Guy (2001). "Internationalization of large-format retailers and leisure providers in western Europe: planning and property impacts." *International Journal of Retail & Distribution Management*, Volume: 29 Number: 10 , Page: 452 - 461.

17. David Bennett, Paul Forrester, John Hassard (1992). "Market-driven Strategies and the Design of Flexible Production Systems: Evidence from the Electronics Industry."International Journal of Operations and Production, Management,Volume: 12, Number: 2. Page : 8 - 11.

18. Donald Skilling (1996). "Beyond the quick fix: how to manage more effectively in the heart of change." *Industrial and Commercial Training,* Volume: 28, Number: 4, Page: 3 - 7.

19. Everard Tarascio (1997). "Business critical messaging." *Journal: Information Management & Computer Security,* Volume: 5, Number: 4, Page: 149- 152.

20. Ewen Kinnear (1997). "Is there any magic in cross-docking?." *Supply Chain Management: An International Journal,* Volume: 2, Number: 2, Page: 49 - 52.

21. Goran Svensson (2003). "The bullwhip effect in intra-organizational echelon." *International Journal of Physical Distribution & Logistics Management,* Volume: 33, Number: 2, Page: 103 - 131.

22. Herbert Kotzab (1999). "Improving supply chain performance by efficient consumer response? A critical comparison of existing ECR approaches." *Journal of Business and Industrial Marketing,* Volume: 14, Number: 5, Page: 364 - 377.

23. Jan C Fransoo, Marc J.F. Wouters (2000). "Measuring the bullwhip effect in the supply chain." *Supply Chain Management: An International Journal,* Volume: 5, Number: 2, Page: 78 - 89 53.

24. Jan Olhager, Erik Selldin (2003). "Enterprise resource planning survey of Swedish manufacturing firms." *European Journal of Operational Research,* Volume: 4, Number 4, Page 365 - 373.

25. Jan Holmström, Ari-Pekka Hameri (1999). "The dynamics of consumer response A quest for the attractors of supply chain demand"*International Journal of Operations Production Management,*Volume: 19 Number: 10 Page: 993 1010

26. Joshua Bamfield (1994). "Technological Management Learning: The Adoption of Electronic Data Interchange by Retailers." *International Journal of Retail & Distribution Management,* Volume: 22 , Number: 2, Page: 3 - 11.

27. J.A.N. Bamfield (1994). "Implementing EDI: Problems in Managing Retail / Supplier Relationships by Technology." *Logistics Information Management.* Volume: 7, Number: 1, Page: 7 - 10.

28. Julia Hanna (2004), "Ground-Floor Opportunities for Retail in India." *Harvard Business Review* from http://hbswk.hbs.edu/pubitem.jhtml?id=4072&t=special_reports_india 2004.

29. Leo R Vijayasarathy, Michael L Tyler (1997). "Adoption factors and electronic data interchange use: a survey of retail companies." *International Journal of Retail & Distribution Management,* Volume: 25, Number: 9, Page: 286 - 292.

30. Leigh Sparks, Beverly A Wagner (2003). "Retail exchanges: a research agenda." *Supply Chain Management: An International Journal,* Volume: 8, Number: 3, Page:201 -208.

31. Marco Iansiti and Roy Levien (2004). "Strategy for Small Fish."*Harvard Business Review* from http://hbswk.hbs.edu/ item. jhtml?id=4331&t=innovation.

32. Mariano Corso, Antonella Martini, Emilio Paolucci, Luisa Pellegrini (2003)."Knowledge management configurations in Italian small-to-medium enterprises."*Integrated Manufacturing Systems,* Volume: 14, Number: 1, Page: 46 - 52.

33. Mark Peterson, Jeffrey E McGee (2000). "Survivors of "W-day": an assessment of the impact of Wal-Mart's invasion of small town retailing communities."*International Journal of Retail & Distribution Management,* Volume: 28, Number: 4, Page: 170 - 180.

34. Majed Al-Mashari, Abdullah Al-Mudimigh, Mohamed Zairi (2002). "Enterprise resource planning: A taxonomy of critical factors." *European Journal of Operational Research,* Volume: 12, Number: 3, Page 242-253.

35. Melih Kirlidog (1996). "Information technology transfer to a developing country."*Information Technology & People*, Volume: 9, Number: 3, Page: 55 -84 -54.

36. Michael J Gallivan, Jim Eynon, Arun Rai (2003). "The challenge of knowledge management systems: Analyzing the dynamic processes underlying performance improvement initiatives." *Information Technology & People,* Volume: 16, Number:3, Page: 326- 352.

37. Michael S Spencer, Dale S Rogers, Patricia J Daugherty (1994). "JIT Systems and External Logistics Suppliers." *International Journal of Operations & Production Management,* Volume: 14, Number: 6, Page: 60 - 74.

38. Marilyn M Helms, Lawrence P Ettkin, Sharon Chapman (2000). "Supply chain forecasting - Collaborative forecasting supports supply chain management." *Business Process Management Journal,* Volume: 6, Number: 5, Page: 392- 407.

39. Navdeep Aggarwal, Raghbir Singh (2004). "Market orientation in Indian organizations: an empirical study." *Marketing Intelligence & Planning,* Volume: 22 Number: 7 Page: 700 -715.

40. Neelam Kinra (1995). "Strategic dimensions in marketing planning: large versus small/medium companies in the Indian television market." *Marketing Intelligence & Planning Journal,* Volume: 13, Number: 4, Page: 34 - 44.

41. Nynke Faber, Rene Marinus, B.M. de Koster, Steef L vande (2002). "Linking warehouse complexity to warehouse planning and control structure: An exploratorystudy of the use of warehouse management information systems." *International Journal of Physical Distribution & Logistics Management,* Volume: 32, Number: 5, Page: 381 - 395.

42. Peter Gilmour (1999). "A strategic audit framework to improve supply chain performance." *The Journal of Business and Industrial Marketing,* Volume: 14, Number: 5, Page: 355 - 366.

43. Philip R.S. Wilson, Steve J Fathers (1989)."Distribution - The Contract Approach."*International Journal of physical Distribution & Logistics Management,* Volume: 19, Number: 6.

44. Piyush Kumar Sinha, Arindam Banerjee (2004). "Store choice behaviour in an evolving market." *International Journal of Retail & Distribution,* Volume: 32, Number: 10, Page: 482- 494

45. Reed Moyer (1991). "A bargain theory of pricing." *European Journal of Marketing,* Volume: 5, Number: 4, Page: 161- 167.

46. Remko I van Hoek, Alan Harrison, Martin Christopher (2001). "Measuring agile capabilities in the supply chain." *International Journal of Operations & Production Management,* Volume: 21, Number: 1, Page: 126 - 148.

47. Richard P Vlosky, Paul M Smith, David T Wilson (1994). "Electronic DataInterchange Implementation Strategies: A Case Study." *The Journal of Business andIndustrial Marketing,* Volume: 9 ,Number: 4, Page: 5 - 18.

48. Ritu Lohtia, Ramesh Subramaniam (2000). "Structural transformation of the Japanese retail distribution system." *The Journal of Business and Industrial Marketing,* Volume: 15, Number:5, Page: 323 - 339.

49. Sarah Jane Johnston (2004). "What Drives Supply Chain Behavior?" *Harvard Business Review* from http://hbswk.hbs.edu/item.jhtml?id= 4170&t = operations.

50. S. M. Disney, D.R. Towill (2003). "Vendor-managed inventory and bullwhip reduction in a two-level supply chain." *International Journal of Operations & Production Management,* Volume: 23, Number: 6, Page: 625 - 651.

51. Samuel W Jimba (1999)."Information technology and underdevelopment in the Third World." *Library Review,* Volume: 4,8 Number: 2, Page: 79 - 83.

52. Sanjay K Bhattacharyya, Zillur Rahman (2003). "Why large local conglomerates maynot work in emerging markets." *European Business Review,* Volume: 15, Number: 2, Page: 105 - 115.

53. Sharon M Davidson, Amy Rummel (2000). "Retail changes associated with Wal- Mart's entry into Maine." *International Journal of Retail & Distribution Management,* Volume: 28, Number: 4, Page: 162 -169.

54. Siriginidi Subba Rao (2000). "E-commerce: the medium is the mart." *New Library World,* Volume: 101, Number: 2, Page: 53 -59

55. Stephen J Arnold, John Fernie (2000). "Wal-Mart in Europe: prospects for the UK."*International Marketing Review,* Volume: 17, Number: 4, Page: 416 - 432.

56. Susan A Shaw, Donald J Nisbet, John A Dawson (2001). "Economies of Scale in UK Supermarkets: Some Preliminary Findings." *International Journal of Retail & Distribution Management,* Volume: 15, Number: 3, Page 272-280.

57. Steve V Walton, Jatinder N.D. Gupta.(1999). "Electronic data interchange for process change in an integrated supply chain." *International Journal of Operations & Production Management,* Volume: 19, Number: 4, Page: 372 - 388.

58. Tim McLaren, Milena Head, Yufei Yuan (2002). "Supply chain collaboration alternatives: understanding the expected costs and benefits." *Internet Research: Electronic Networking Applications and Policy,* Volume: 12, Number: 4, Page: 348- 364.

59. Toni M. Somers a, Klara G. Nelson b (2003). "The impact of strategy and integration."

60. Michman, Ronald, and Edward Mazze, -Specialty stores, Marketing Triumphs and Blunders. Westport,CT: Quorum Books, 2001.

61. Food for Thought: Discount Stores Eat into Supermarket, Drug Store Sales, Chain Store Age, May 2000, p. 49ones,Ken, and Michael Pearce. "The Geography of Markets: Spatial Analysis for Retailers." Ivey Business Journal 63, no. 3, March-April,.1999.

62. Salvaneschi, Luigi, and Camille Akin, Eds. Location, Location, Location: How to select the best site for Your Business. Psi Successful Business Library, 1996.

63. Kabachnick, Terri, Retailers Need to Be Aware of the Trends Transforming Today's Workforce, WWD, Chicago Supplement, May 1999, p.28.

64. Jackson, Susan, and Randall Schuler, Managing Human Resources Through Strategic Relationships. 8th ed., Mason. OH: Southwestern, 2003.

65. Noe,Raymond;John Hollenbeck; Barry Gerhart; and Patrick Wright. Human Resource Management, 4th ed. Burr Ridge, IL:Mc Graw Hill Irwin, 2003.

66. Rigby,Darrell; Fredrick Reichheld; ;and Phil Schefter. Avoiding the Four perils of CRM, Harvard Business Review, Feb. 2002.

67. Crosby,John,V.Cycles, Trends, and Turning Points: Practical Marketing and Sales Forecasting Techniques: NTC Publishing Group, 1999.

68. Dussart,C.'Category Management: Strengths, Limits and Developments." European Management Journal 16, No.1 1998, pp.50-62.

69. Barr,Vilma and Katherine Field, Stores: Retail Displays and Design, PBC International, 1999.

70. Bell,Judith, and Kat Ternus, Silent Selling: Practices and Effective Strategies for Visual Merchandising, 2nd Ed., New York, Fairchild Books, Nov. 2000. Underhill, Paco. Why We Buy: The Science of Shopping. New York, Simon & Schuster, 2000.

